Shades of Victory

SOUL-STIRRING STORIES OF
TRIALS AND TRIUMPHS

The Shades of Victory Sisterhood

Contents

Acknowledgements   v

Dedication   vii

Shades of Victory   ix

Victory in my Marriage   1

Victory Over Imposter Syndrome   9

Walk in Victory   15

Victory in Seeking God First   27

The Victorious Journey   39

Victory Over My Enemy   43

A Victorious Faith Walk   57

Healing Victory   67

Victory Over Family Matters   77

Victory in Community   87

Victory Over Abuse and Grief   103

Epilogue   117

Meet the Authors   119

Acknowledgements

We thank God for guiding us throughout our journey and giving us the strength to accomplish this important mission. Through His grace, we are blessed to share our tales of victory, with hopes of inspiring others.

A special thanks to the Fearless Storytellers, whose unwavering support was instrumental in bringing this project to life, allowing us to tell our stories and empower women near and far.

Dedication

This book is dedicated to women who dare to live a victorious life.

Shades of Victory

The Shades of Victory Book Club is more than a gathering of friends to discuss literature; it's a sisterhood. We laugh hard, and sometimes we cry hard, but we never have to apologize for who we are. An abundance of acceptance among the women in our group creates a safe space that allows us to be authentic. Protecting this kinship requires harmony, understanding, togetherness, and community. Whether we agree or agree to disagree, we don't allow the differences to affect our sisterhood.

Shades of Victory includes amazing women from diverse backgrounds who share a common factor: Victory in Jesus Christ. Although our personalities and circumstances look different—that's what creates the shades—we have established a genuine sisterhood where we can uplift and encourage one another. Each sister brings unique qualities that add value to the group.

Danielle Mack not only co-leads the group, but is also my prayer partner. She played an integral role in getting the book club started. When I presented the idea to her she encouraged me to move forward. Inviting ladies to join us as we stepped out in faith to build our community, was her way of saying, "I am all in". Today, she helps organize events and provides structure. Because of her peaceful demeanor, everyone enjoys being around her. Danielle is a foodie, so her job is to find good restaurants whenever we travel.

Danielle Anderson is loving and soft-spoken with a heart of humility. Her words of encouragement build up the women in our group. She listens attentively to the concerns of others and responds biblically with words of wisdom. Her laughter and smile make her a joy to be around.

Tiffany Coleman is an original book club member who is supportive and inspirational. Her caring and empathetic personality makes the book club a safe space. If there is a need, she is ready to step in and help. Opening her home for book club meetings is a joy.

Lisa Collins is an original book club member who is thoughtful, generous, and laid back. Her transparent and nonjudgmental personality allows discussions to be uninhibited. She creates an environment where we can be ourselves, openly sharing our pains and regrets. She is financially savvy and always ready to share her expertise with the group.

Valarie Downing is an original book club member who never takes a seat at the center of attention and always hides in the back or outskirts of photos, but her presence is that of a pillar in our sisterhood. We can count on her to pray, hold our secrets, and respond with Godly wisdom. She listens with a heart of grace and never hesitates to celebrate the goodness of God. She leads by example and teaches us how to be grateful in tough situations.

Betty Lodge is an original book club member and one of the people who encouraged me to step out and start the book club. From the beginning, she believed that the club would unite women through discussing life issues. She brings a sense of strength and resilience to the club. She speaks the truth in a way that doesn't crush our spirits but empowers us to do better. She is a fighter and encourages the ladies to be strong.

Joyce Talbert is insightful and jovial. She has a way of entertaining the group effortlessly, bringing lots of laughter and joy to every gathering. Her love for Christ is evident in the way she serves others. Because of her creativity, we rely on her to help us with fresh marketing concepts.

Jennifer Taylor is laid back and observant. She shares ideas and insights in any given discussion. Finding commonality among people is one of her greatest character strengths. Sacrificial is the adjective that comes to mind when I think about Jennifer. She travels from Texas to attend our meetings and is willing to serve wherever needed. Making her famous grits when we travel is her chosen assignment.

Tiffany Temple brings thought-provoking questions to our book club. She challenges us to grow and dream. Her adventurous personality adds an element of suspense and fun to our gatherings. Taking pictures is one of her hobbies, so we count on her to document our events and manage the website.

Tawanda Weatherspoon has a big, tender heart. She adds a spark of energy and adventure to our book club. With her lighthearted, youthful spirit, she brings fun, creativity, and spontaneity. She organizes our travel events and manages our budget.

To commemorate the 10-year anniversary of our Shades of Victory Book Club, we thought it would be fitting to write our own book together. The purpose of sharing our stories is to give you, the reader, hope as you navigate your own struggles. Remember, it doesn't matter how you start; it's how you finish. Life can be hard, but God is always good. "But thanks be to God! He gives us the victory through our Lord Jesus Christ" (1 Corinthians 15:57).

May the differing shades of our stories inspire you to your ultimate victory!

Monica Goree
Shades of Victory Book Club Visionary

"The decision to stay in the marriage was rooted in my obedience to God, not my desire to be with Donald."

Victory in my Marriage

MONICA GOREE

Why did you stay? Everyone wants to know my answer to that question after reading my husband's book. *Living Proof* addresses his past drug addiction and has people asking me some tough questions: How did you put up with this man? Were you afraid? Did you think he would ever be free? Since the journey out of hardship and addiction was a long one, the best way to answer those questions is to start from the beginning.

In July 1985, my sister invited me to be her guest at her husband's family reunion. Sitting at a picnic table filled with his aunts, uncles, and cousins, I locked eyes with Donald. From that point, it was on. He asked for my phone number, and we started hanging out. After a few dates, the excitement wore off and we stopped talking. Several months later, we ran into each other at a restaurant and began communicating again. The second time around, things felt different.

We started off as friends, talking about anything and everything, sharing our dreams and fears. Our friendship seemed natural, and a romantic connection bloomed. Laughter was always part of our conversations, and we were comfortable sharing our pains and frustrations. Donald liked to read and was outgoing and fun. He made me laugh—he still does. We enjoyed doing many of the same things: attending sporting events and concerts, walking, traveling, and hanging out with family and friends. I encouraged him to dream big. In fact, his business, D's Cleaning Service, was birthed with a little nudge from me.

On Christmas Eve 1987, Donald proposed to me at my home in front of my family. I happily accepted his proposal. Since I was pregnant at the time with our son, Brennan, we delayed the wedding until after he was born. The delay was partially because I wanted to fit into the wedding dress and partly because I wanted to be sure I wasn't operating on pregnancy emotions. I wanted no doubts this was the man I wanted to marry. We married on November 11, 1988.

Life was good for the first two years. During that time, we welcomed another baby, our sweet daughter, Brandi. However, when year three rolled around, things began to change. Little did I know, an underlying current was about to sweep over our happy life and with it a hardship I wasn't prepared to handle.

When I met Donald, he smoked weed (and I won't lie—I smoked it with him). Occasionally, he snorted cocaine. However, I did not discover until three years into our marriage he was also smoking crack. At first, he convinced me he was in control of this habit. I believed him until the money started getting funny. When the rent checks started bouncing, I knew he'd lost control, and his addiction was more serious than I cared to admit. Every time I confronted Donald, he had good excuses. Since he wouldn't tell me the truth, I called his friends' wives, and they confirmed drug use among their men was out of control. After my investigation, I approached him. With the information I presented, he had no choice but to admit he was using drugs. The confession relieved him because he no longer had to hide his activities from me.

With the crack epidemic all over the news and my husband a part of it, I was ashamed. I tried to deal with it alone because I didn't want anyone to know. Eventually, I told his mother, but that backfired because he now felt abundant freedom to do as he pleased. He began staying out late at night, and when he got really strung, he lost his job. He'd go on binges and be absent for days at a time. Many times, I wondered if he would even come home. I didn't know if he was dead or alive.

All the madness was overwhelming. After one of his binges, I was fed up and decided to put him out. I called my cousin whose husband was a handyman and asked him to change all the locks. My cousin was fed up too and ready to see him go. (You know how family is—we stick together.) My cousin's husband looked at me and said, "Look, I'm not about to change all these locks just for you to give him a key. If you give him a key after I change all these locks, I'm not going to do anything for you again." Then reality set in, and I decided not to change the locks. A part of me wanted to let go; the other part was thinking about my kids.

Brennan and Brandi were my blessings from the Lord, and I did everything in my power to shield them from the disarray. Although I wanted more children, my dream of a large family had faded after my daughter was born because I didn't want to bring any more children into our chaotic world. At the time of Donald's addiction, the kids were too young to understand what was happening. Instead of focusing on the neglect, financial strain, and emotional trauma I was experiencing, I spent my time reading to the children at night, cooking meals for them, and doing other extracurricular activities to enhance their lives. They loved their father, who loved them as much as he could, given the circumstances. Because my son was older, he was more aware that something was off which prompted me to run interference when it came to his dad's absence. I refused to allow what was going on with Donald to affect the children any more than it had to. (Today, for the most part, my kids have good memories from their childhood with their dad.)

I still wrestled with the desire to leave. While Donald was gone on one of his binges, I found an apartment and was just waiting for the next opportunity to gather my kids and go. I didn't tell a soul about my plan—not my mom, not my friends, not even my kids. I figured I would just wait him out and disappear the next time he disappeared. But God knew how to stop me in my tracks. One day my mother's friend called and told me she had a dream that I was trying to leave my husband. She advised me not to leave. She went on to say he was just a "diamond in the rough" and to hang in there. I hardly knew this woman, yet the Lord was speaking through her because she had no way of knowing my plans. I broke down on the phone and cried. I was angry! I was caught between two places. I wanted to move on with my life—a life that did not include Donald. I was angry because I was carrying most of the weight when he chose drugs. I was angry because my family had to help me, and it wasn't their responsibility. I was angry because Donald wasn't providing. Honestly, I was angry at God because He wouldn't release me from this marriage. However, I obeyed the Lord.

My husband's drug addiction made me seek the Lord and get rooted in the

Word of God. When Donald and I met, I was attending a church that didn't talk about salvation in the way I understand it now. I read the Bible but didn't make it relevant to my life. Going to church was more of a ritual, and I later realized that I didn't have a relationship with God. Trauma drove me to my knees, and I began to cry out to God for help. My mother's friend invited me to a spirit-filled church service; her husband was the pastor. This church was definitely different from where I attended. They preached from the Bible about practical living and about Jesus being not only our Savior but our friend. They also taught me I could find answers to life's issues through the Bible. Needless to say, I joined this church in 1992 and began leaning on the Lord. I started reading the Bible for myself and understanding the difference between attending church and having a relationship with the Lord. One Sunday, after the pastor preached about how God can change people's lives and give them peaceful minds, I walked up to the altar and said, "Lord, I surrender my life to you." My connection with the Lord was ignited that day.

After that, whenever a threat came, I looked to the Lord who had promised to take care of me. He always provided. Whenever there was a financial shortage, the Lord sent people to help because He promised to "supply all of my needs according to His glorious riches" (Philippians 4:19). Once as I questioned the Lord about how I was going to pay my bills, He sent a woman that day to pay them all. God showed me time and time again He was with me.

Occasionally, I received threats from drug dealers because Donald owed them money. One day, a drug dealer contacted me, looking for my husband. He threatened to blow up my house with my kids and me inside. Hearing those words should have frightened me, but instead, it made me angry. I told that drug dealer, "Don't mess with me!" He taunted me, "What are you gonna do?!" I told him I had holy angels all around my house, and if he came near my home, he was going to find himself in a lot of trouble. He told me I was crazy. A few days after that encounter, the dealer had an argument with someone and got shot. Two weeks later, he called and asked me to forgive him for threatening me. He asked me to pray for him, and I did. Even in the midst of the chaos, God was cleansing my heart and teaching me to see people through His eyes. Drug dealers need to know about Jesus too, so I began to share the word of God with this gentleman. That incident led him to the Lord.

Even with such great testimonies, I was still frustrated about staying with Donald. The decision to stay was rooted in my obedience to God, not my desire to be with Donald. The turning point in my struggle with staying came in 1995. I told the Lord I couldn't stay in the marriage without Him. I didn't trust Donald, but I trusted God. I told God if He wanted me to stay, He had to help me mentally because there was no way I could do it on my own. As God helped me change my focus from Donald to Him, things began to change.

Now, let me say this, I am not a prophet, and I never claimed to be, but the Lord began giving me prophetic words to share with Donald. Once, I told him if he went wherever he planned to go that night, he'd regret it. The Lord had shown me police cars everywhere. He asked me how I knew that. I was simply telling him what the Lord was showing me. The next day, he told me there was an incident at that location, the police were called, and several people were arrested. He was glad he did not make his usual visit that night. On another occasion, I told Donald I had a vision someone had given him a car, but he didn't believe me. The following morning, I had another vision that once he got that car, he would lose it in exchange for drugs. Donald called me crazy. He said he wasn't giving away the car that was given to him. Within seven days, everything the Lord showed me had come to pass. The next vision I had was of Donald preaching from a wheelchair. I told him that would be his fate if he didn't get his life together. God used those visions to grab Donald's attention. I have never had such clear visions or prophetic words for anyone else since then.

Donald wanted to be clean, and he knew God was the only way that would happen. Church was a big part of his upbringing, so it was natural for him to attend church. He attended services throughout his addiction and would go to the altar on a regular basis. Sometimes he would have the preacher pour oil on him from head to toe, fall out, get up, and say, "Oh, I'm free!" That would last all of a couple of days or so. He even went to rehab a couple of times. I fell for it at first, but after a while, I'd just look at him like, *Oh, okay. . .yeah, right.* I wasn't taking him seriously. I knew he wasn't really done with that part of his life. He'd go back and forth with me, asking when I was going to believe him. I didn't know when I would believe him. I felt like when he was truly drug-free, I would know.

On April 7, 1997, he came to me and said the Lord had spoken to him about going to seminary school in Baton Rouge. He knew leaving St. Louis was the only way he would escape his addiction. I replied, "Okay, when are you leaving?" He said he wanted to leave the next day. I helped him pack because I wanted him out of my hair. He asked me if I would move with him, and I told him I needed to pray about that. My entire support system was in St. Louis. I figured he could attend school in Baton Rouge, then return to St. Louis, and we could start over. He was adamant about the kids and me moving with him, but he also understood that he had put us through a lot.

After he left, I was relieved. I don't know if that feeling of relief was due to him being free of drugs or me being free of him. While he was gone, I had time to pray and seek the Lord for answers. Donald asked me to come for a visit in May to get a feel for the city in hopes I would move with him. I came and felt a sense of peace about moving. I believed Donald was drug-free and ready to live for God. After moving to Baton Rouge, we opened a joint bank account. This was a big step towards rebuilding trust in our relationship because years prior when Donald started messing up our money, I had opened a bank account with only my name on it. We both knew this was a definitive turning point. We were on our way to victory in our marriage!

The journey moving forward wasn't always easy because there were plenty of hurts to overcome, but fighting for our marriage was worth it. Donald became a great husband and father and provided for us financially and led us spiritually. He is such a blessing to me now. I no longer worry if he will return every time he leaves the house. He also works with men in prison and homeless shelters who are battling substance abuse. Because of his past addiction, he can truly connect with people and understand their pain.

Donald was not the only one who had to conquer the addiction. I, too, had to overcome the trauma I endured during that time. I was traumatized and didn't realize it. In the middle of the battle, I could only think about survival. It wasn't until I fell on my knees and began to pray that change came. And to be clear, the change started with me. God softened my heart towards Donald and the drug dealers. Like I said earlier, the victory came when I shifted my focus from Donald to Jesus. I recognize now how God used those trying times to build my character.

When I tell my story, I am very careful not to oversimplify how things worked out. Not everyone could do what I did. I was only able to do it because

I knew I was hearing from the Lord. It wasn't easy, but I knew I was *called* to do it. God ordained me for this assignment. Throughout my journey, I was constantly leaning on God because the victory didn't happen overnight. There were plenty of times when I wasn't happy-go-lucky. In fact, there were many years of tears. It was three years before a change came. But when it came, it came swiftly. My husband was a drug addict one day, and the next day he wasn't. It was God who did it!

Victory doesn't come in a one-size-fits-all box. There is no blanket advice I give people in similar circumstances that I think will solve their problems. I realize desperate people are willing to take advice from anyone they think is qualified to give it, but that usually results in confusion. My advice is for them to seek the Lord for themselves. If they aren't, no amount of advice given will soothe their situation. I encourage them to go into a quiet place with God and listen for His voice. I also suggest they read the Bible because the answers to life's problem are found in it.

So, to answer everyone's question, Why did you stay? I stayed because of the Lord. If my mother's friend had not called me on that cold winter night and told me to stick it out, I would have been gone. It wasn't easy nor was it my choice to endure something so painful. Even now, there are moments when I think, *Wow, I can't believe I got through that*, but I did. Life with God is the game changer. The Lord did it for us, and He can do it for anyone. Donald and I are living proof, and we have victory in our marriage!

"Stand in your power, which means not allowing anyone, not even yourself, to diminish your significance in the spaces God has ordained for you."

Victory Over Imposter Syndrome

DANIELLE MACK

For a long time, I believed I needed to present a perfect persona. From the outside, everything seemed to align — a happy marriage, a beautiful home, countless professional achievements, a talented daughter, and a dream job. But looking perfect and being perfect are worlds apart. The reality of balancing all of these things comes with its own set of challenges. The truth is, perfection doesn't exist for anyone. We all face challenges and embark on daily journeys filled with unexpected twists and turns and road bumps along the way.

Looking back, it's clear I had a case of "oldest child syndrome". I was the compliant child, constantly striving to please. Although I navigated my teenage years with a few spurts of rebellion, I generally followed the rules. I grew up in a very religious household, and there were many do's and don'ts. My father was a minister, and my mother was equally involved in church, so religion and faith were ingrained deeply in our family dynamic and values. At times, my upbringing led me to judge others, holding them to standards similar to what was set for me. It took me a long time to break free from that and foster a more inclusive and understanding mindset. **I had to shift my mentality.**

My parents took great care of us. They both sacrificed so my siblings and I had what we needed and some of the things we wanted. We went on family vacations annually and my brother, sister and I maintain stable relationships with one another today. While my childhood may not have been traumatic, it was definitely strict and sometimes very rigid.

My brother, sister and I can now laugh about the strict rules we endured. At that time growing up, we weren't necessarily happy about not being able to do all of "the things", however we maintain an appreciation for our parents looking out for us.

Even as I progressed into adulthood, that "oldest child syndrome" was still present. I always felt the need to set an example by aiming for perfection, sticking to the rules and not making major waves. It was often difficult to be vulnerable and share with others my shortcomings.

I remember hearing a message one Sunday during church that resonated deeply and freed me from checking the boxes and feeling the need to be "perfect." I wanted a relationship with God that didn't require all the conditions I learned growing up. I needed to be able to come before Him, unhidden with all my blemishes. I knew I represented Christ, but I wasn't perfect. We all have imperfections.

Let me first begin by acknowledging the abundance of blessings and favor that have graced my journey. I have been blessed beyond measure and I'm not afraid to proudly state it. Now there is an old adage that says, "people see your glory, but they don't know your story", and I deeply relate. The inside scoop is that at my core – I am an introvert, often feel judged and have struggled with imposter syndrome. Despite this, life has ushered me into roles that required a shift, a push sometimes into the limelight, encouraging the leader within me to emerge and push beyond my comfort zone. Thankfully, I have always had a circle of mentors, champions and prayer warriors rooting for me. And for that, I am grateful.

The appearance of success can sometimes be misleading, painting a façade that appears like I have it all together. From my memorable college days, where I landed a prized student job, to earning a coveted spot on our University's homecoming court not once, but twice, and pledging my beloved sorority, I encountered many days of insecurity and disappointment. Many thought I had everything figured out, but in reality, I was often self-conscious, constantly judging myself and feeling like others were scrutinizing me too.

One thing I have appreciated is having a circle of spiritual women of faith that are by my side. The ladies of the Shades of Victory book club definitely encouraged me. If there's ever an issue, we work through it and pray about it. I've become much more vulnerable in the group. I share my struggles, like navigating parenting a teenager or a fear I may encounter before a tough conversation or big presentation. I know it's a safe space. However, I wasn't always one to share anything. I allowed the other ladies to share things with me. I was eager to help and support them, but I always found it hard for me to trust and open up to others the way they opened up to me.

Being an introvert, building deep connections with other women has always been a bit of a challenge for me. However, over time, I've learned the important value of opening up and sharing my experiences. This journey towards personal growth not only helped me come into my own but also naturally progressed into guiding young women through formal and informal mentorship who might be facing similar challenges. I've noticed that, like many introverts, there's a tendency to withdraw after social interactions. Yet, I've found that making an intentional effort to reconnect and follow up is crucial for nurturing relationships. Embracing vulnerability has been instrumental in helping me break out of my shell, allowing for more meaningful connections with others.

Being behind the scenes was not only my comfort zone, but also my clear preference. Supporting the person in charge with their vision as number two was my natural niche. However, when the opportunity for a promotion at work presented itself, it was my husband James' unwavering support and encouragement that became a defining factor. He saw potential in me that I often overlooked, and without his belief in my capabilities, I might not have taken that leap. Despite being thrust front and center, I was plagued with Imposter Syndrome, filled with self-doubt, and questioned if I was qualified or smart enough. I didn't want to steer the ship; I yearned to be the one supporting the leader. Yet, I trust that God places us in specific roles for profound reasons. With my husband's encouragement and my acceptance of this leadership role, I embarked on a transformative journey, learning more about myself and beginning to overcome my self-doubt.

One of the first steps to overcoming Imposter Syndrome is acknowledging it. You have to own your voice, your path, and your goals. You have to believe in your own strength. It's also important to know where you fall short and be okay with it. Everyone has their strengths and weaknesses. No matter how minuscule you believe your contribution is, your voice matters. The part you play matters. It's easy to focus on what you don't do well. Know that it's okay to delegate tasks to those who might be better suited for them. Successful collaboration and growth rely on recognizing your value and the unique contributions you bring, while empowering others around you.

Tackling imposter syndrome is already challenging enough, but navigating it as a Black woman in the corporate world introduces additional layers of complexity, making it even more difficult to overcome. In certain professional spaces, I've felt the need to 'morph' or code-switch, a practice that sometimes leaves me walking on eggshells, wary of expressing my true feelings for fear of being perceived or treated differently. This code-switching, an unsaid rule in professional dynamics, has been a challenging yet essential part of my career progression. It's a bittersweet realization, as I've witnessed firsthand brighter, more confident professionals and colleagues who struggled or were not willing to master with this aspect and faced professional setbacks.

As I advanced in my role, I discovered my voice and unexpectedly gained recognition as an expert in my field, pushing me further out of my comfort zone. Leading a team and needing to deliver results helped me confront and push through my Imposter Syndrome. This journey taught me the importance of being assertive and confident in my abilities. While it's a complex balance of maintaining authenticity and adapting to professional environments, I've come to see this adaptability not just as a survival mechanism, but as a form of diplomacy and a key to career advancement. I'm also acutely aware of how this delicate navigation impacts the example I set for my daughter, Autumn, underlining the importance of resilience and integrity along with every step.

So many people have been cheerleaders for me and believed in me, but I haven't always believed in myself. My habit of doubting my abilities was exhausting and caused tremendous anxiety. I've worked diligently to get where I am. I have friends and colleagues who have earned several degrees, and they have not been as fortunate as I have been in my professional life. Due to that fact, I find myself downplaying my accomplishments, and I know I have to stop doing that. My mom has always been and still remains one of my biggest cheerleaders, encouraging me and celebrating the small victories that I sometimes brush aside. When I receive praise for my blessings, I am learning to say, "To God Be the Glory."

I have mentors who directly challenge me by asking why I don't believe I belong in certain spaces at work. Soon, I began standing in my power, which helped me get past some of the effects of Imposter Syndrome. If you struggle with Imposter Syndrome, don't beat yourself up. I am victorious in this arena because those moments when I feel inadequate are the days I lean deeper into prayer. I remind myself of what God's Word says about me. Stand in your power, which means not allowing anyone, not even yourself, to diminish your significance in the spaces God has ordained for you. Whether you're navigating the complexities of the corporate world or embracing your own understanding of faith, know that your voice and presence are significant and make a difference.

10 When Jesus stood up, He said to her, "Woman, where are they? Has no one condemned you?" 11 "No one, Lord,"[a] she answered. "Neither do I condemn you," said Jesus. "Go, and from now on do not sin anymore."][b] John 8:10-11

Walk in Victory

JOYCE WEATHERSPOON-TALBERT

I grew up in Scotlandville, in a white two-story, four-bedroom, and one-bathroom house. I lived with my mom and dad and six other siblings however I didn't see my dad as much, in fact whenever he did come home it was like a holiday because he would give us money to go to the corner store. He was funny with a raspy voice from smoking for so many years and he loved to kick up his hills and dance with us kids, those are the best memories I have of him being home with us. But I also recall it seemed he would disappear and reappear at odd times. There were small arguments between my parents but nothing ever violent. My mom was fun, creative, and determined. She did volunteer work in the community, and she loved children. My home life at that time was somewhat happy, I loved that house on Rosenwald Street, and I can still see it today. But I can also recall the molesting starting at that time as well. Amazing how beauty and horror can exist in the same space. At the age of seven, our house burned down, and we were forced to move. From the time I was nine years old until adulthood my family and I lived on Pimpernel Street.

My parents divorced when I was nine years old. When they divorced, I felt like my dad divorced us too. Many times, we would call and ask to spend the weekend with him, he would say yes to picking us up but 1Q majority of the time he would not show up or call and I can still remember peaking out the window until midnight waiting for him to come. Rejection left a huge impact on my life.

When my mother met Melvin, he was a big man, we thought he was fun, and strong. He drove 18-wheeler trucks for a living, how he met my mom I don't know. Melvin came to live with us and at first, everything seemed great until the arguments started. There were heated arguments at first that soon turned physical. When my mom said they were getting married all of us kids were against it, and we wanted him to leave and said as much to my mom but she didn't listen. The domestic violence was traumatic. It was years of violence, running away to live with family, I was so scared most times I would hide in closets because it wasn't safe to be around them. I was never smart in school, an average student at best. Most of the time, I slept at school because I was too afraid to sleep at home. Between the molestation and the domestic violence, I was trying to survive the nights. By the time I was 13, I was ready to catch a plane somewhere and never return. This was my life.

I've experienced some childhood trauma. I was molested for ten years. That traumatic episode affected me moving forward in life. My parents were divorced and both remarried. After the divorce, my father just walked away. I wish I could say that my father was still there, but he wasn't. We couldn't talk about my father, much less, say the word, Daddy around my mother. If we did, my mother would go into this long, drawn-out rant about how he left her with seven kids.

We grew up going to church, my dad was a deacon and later became a pastor. He also remarried but his wife didn't like us very much. I believed in God, always thought He was real, but the way people acted in church around us appeared fake. I first heard the gospel of Jesus Christ when I was 16. We were at my older sister's bridal shower when she and her friends began witnessing to the guests. I heard their words and asked the Lord to forgive and save me. With no one around to teach me what salvation meant I was left to myself and drifted on my own, which I did for nearly fifteen years.

By the time I was 28, I began having an affair with a 42-year-old man that I worked with. I always knew it was wrong. My family knew him because he'd come to family events with me. But no one knew that he was married. I was foolishly doing my own thing.

He and I were both avid readers. We connected with each other based on our love for books. We'd talk about the things we read. One day, he suggested to me to read the Bible and that it was the greatest book ever written. Oddly enough, he said this to me after the affair had begun. We had been several years into the affair at this point. I was 32 years old.

I had no idea what I was getting myself into. I agreed to his suggestion, and I began at the beginning, with the book Genesis. As I read the story of this great Creator of all the world, who called men like Noah, Abraham, and Moses I was amazed at what I was reading. I didn't know that as I was reading, seeds were being planted in my heart. I just thought I was reading a book. Nine months into reading the Bible, I decided, okay, that's enough of that, and I moved on.

I felt so comfortable with him during the affair, in fact he was the first person I had ever talked to about my childhood trauma. One night, he came over and got into bed. He put his hand underneath the pillow and felt the knives I had placed there. Sometimes, I had moments in the middle of the night when I couldn't move. I could hear the doorknob turning. I'd have these nightmares that paralyzed me, and I couldn't move, I would have cold sweats and wake up shaking. When I could move, I'd always get up, grab a knife, and put it underneath my pillow. When he raised the pillow, he saw about 5 or 6 knives. He said, "Whatever it is, you have to talk about it." That was the first time I ever spoke about molestation. I never said anything to anyone before because of the shame I felt. I thought people would judge me, but he didn't. Moments like that connected us even more.

We never get away with anything, his wife almost caught us once. We were going somewhere in my car and were stopped at a light. She was on the other side of the intersection. I just knew that was the day. I was nervous because all she had to do was look over and she would see us. Surprisingly her light changed first, and she drove right past us, not seeing us at all because she never looked over. I didn't know how it was possible that God covered us with His mercy in that moment. Not that He approved of what we were doing. I knew God wasn't pleased, but He showed us mercy.

He and I began struggling in our relationship. I was trying to get out. I'd made plans to move to Alabama with a good girlfriend of mine. But things didn't work out. Inadvertently, I became pregnant. At first, I just thought I had a virus. He told me to get checked out. When I told him about the pregnancy, I made it clear that I wouldn't abort the baby; he said he wouldn't have asked me to. I carried her for the full nine months, and she was born in 1999.

The night my daughter was born, I was alone in the hospital. My family had come earlier to be with me. He was there along with my parents. Later on, after everyone had gone home, and it was just me and my baby something unexpected happened. The room was eerily quiet but peaceful. As I lay there, I heard a voice say, "It is time to get your life in order with Me." and all I could say was, "Yes, Sir."

In April 2000, I began attending Bethany church with my older sister. I began to hear the gospel all over again. I repented to Jesus and asked for forgiveness, I surrendered my life to the Lord on Easter Sunday. I started getting to know God. I told my daughter's dad that we had to end the relationship. I was leaving him for God. He understood. I was never in any physical danger of leaving the relationship, it was difficult because of the soul tie we had.

He loved his daughter. He had two teenage sons with his wife. He wanted her to be a part of her brothers' life. She was about to turn a year old when he decided he couldn't hide her any longer. He told me he needed to tell his wife about our daughter. So he did. She was upset and rightfully so. After a while, he brought our daughter to meet his family. His wife also wanted to meet me. I was afraid.

I knew what it was like to grow up without a father. My father was in and out of my life. He was never a promise keeper. I remember praying to God about my daughter's relationship with her father. He didn't need to be a part of my life, but I needed him to be a part of hers. I know how important it is for a child to experience a father's love.

We all met at a park, not too far from a police station. She was a beautiful woman. She told me she forgave me for what I had done. She assured me that she wouldn't harm my daughter and helped me with her. She promised to never punish my daughter because of the situation. She told me and her husband, "You two are responsible for this." I was flooded with shame and regret. I profusely apologized to her. I wish I could say that nothing ever happened between him and I again, but that would be a lie. Many things happened between us more times than I care to speak about. Apples don't fall that far from the tree. I'm my father's daughter.

It took a few years to sever the soul ties with my daughter's father. Breaking those soul ties did not occur without failure. I was trying to escape, but it was just so hard. I kept falling and failing. I cried a great deal. I deeply desired to live a holy life. I wanted to live right for God. I knew I couldn't sleep around and then go to church. The more I attended church and read the scripture, the more I was convicted. This affair was weighing heavy on me.

I had even become suicidal a couple of times. The first time, my daughter was two years old. Falling back into intimacy with her father is what sent me into a suicidal mindset. My daughter was asleep. It had been a day after being intimate with her father again. As she slept, I sat at the kitchen table with a knife. The guilt and shame was overwhelming. Satan kept telling me, You'll never get out. You're doing too much. God hates you. You sinned against Him again, and it's unforgivable. The attack was relentless. As I sat there listening to the voice in my head and absorbing what was said, I decided to cut my wrist and end it. I was so close to doing it. I know it was the Lord who stepped in and stopped me. I put the knife down and walked away.

Things grew intense in the relationship. We were returning from a family vacation in Florida when we got into a horrible car accident. The car flipped over and started rolling. Our daughter was ejected from her seat, as was my mother and sister. My daughter went through a year of reconstructive surgery on her face. She was three years old. I called her dad to tell him what happened, and he was screaming. He put his wife on the phone, and she asked what happened. I told her about the car accident. I had to tell my family that her dad and his wife were coming. This is how my family found out he was married. They loved him before they found out he was married. The news changed everything, and they never saw him the same way after that.

The second time I attempted suicide, my daughter was four years old. I tried it for the same reason. I decided I was going to use pain medication this time. I had about eight pain pills left in the bottle; I took all of them. The voice in my head told me I was just going to sleep, and I did. Then I woke up. Nothing was wrong. There were no side effects. My daughter was at daycare. I got into my car and started driving. I drove three hours away to Monroe, LA, from Baton Rouge. Something told me to go home, so I did. I turned my car around and went back home. People had begun looking for me because I had left my daughter at daycare. My behavior had started getting dangerous. I realized that no one was going to raise my daughter like me. No one would create special childhood memories like I would. I had to be there for her.

God is merciful and full of grace. He's full of love. But I felt that judgment coming if I didn't stop this relationship with my daughter's father. I knew I couldn't live contrary to God's Word. One of my friends told me, "Sometimes you just have to let it bleed. You have to rip the band-aid off and let it hurt." I didn't want to let it hurt, but I'd gotten to a place where I had no choice. I couldn't be intimate like I desired. I couldn't call him because I wanted to talk. It was a conscious decision, but it took some time for me to gain victory over sexual sin with a married man. Before I knew it, it had been six months, then a year…then two years, and so on, when the soul ties were finally breaking. My body had finally stopped craving him. My heart started chasing the Lord. The focus of my life began changing. Walking in my purpose and the call on my life was my soul's craving.

Eventually, I stopped the suicide attempts, and by the time I was 37, we had severed the intimate part of our relationship. Even after I cut off the relationship, he never tried to push. When I said, "No," he understood. It was hard to stop the relationship because I could be myself unapologetically. It was okay to be me when I was with him. It was safe to be me. He accepted who I was just as I was. I could express myself and not be judged, belittled, or ridiculed. I grew up in a negative environment. I wasn't accepted. As a child, I was called horrible names, not by other kids but by adults, but my daughter's father affirmed me. That was the first time I ever heard that I was beautiful.

I never asked him to leave his wife. I felt we were already in the wrong, carrying on like we were, and divorce would only add to it. He had been with her since they were teenagers. They grew up together. She was his first and only wife and the mother of his two sons. His parents had been together for a long time as well. He grew up with the understanding that when you get married, you stay married. He loved his wife. He never downplayed her or spoke ill of her. Sometimes, men and women will talk poorly about their spouses in order to justify their behavior. He didn't do that. He and I remained friends because of our daughter. I never put him on child support because I didn't need to. I never had to buy her anything she needed. I wasn't a single parent. Whatever she needed, he provided.

I wasn't used to fathers being around and involved. My daughter's father came to see her every day.

I asked him, "Shouldn't you be gone by now?"

"Joyce, this is my daughter. I can't leave my daughter. I have to take care of her."

Whenever she'd go to his house to spend time with him and his wife and kids she never came home and told me anything bad about his wife. They'd go shopping and take vacations. She cooked for my daughter and loved her. It was the true mercy and grace of God that his wife loved my daughter just as much as I did. His wife told me she never had a girl, although she always wanted one. She said my daughter called her Nan'na. She deemed herself my daughter's godmother.

His wife and I had become friends. Sometimes, she'd come over and have dinner, and I'd do the same. She was evidence and proof of God's grace. She believed in God and took the Word of God seriously.

In 2017 my daughter's dad went into the hospital for heart surgery, I took my daughter to see him. I was so overwhelmed with shame and guilt of the past I sat outside in the car, but his wife asked me to come up and see him. I didn't want to go inside because I didn't want to intrude. She assured me that everything was good with us and that I didn't have to sit outside in my car. I felt immense guilt and shame. He wasn't the first man I'd had an affair with, and I've had abortions in the past as a result. I felt that if anyone deserved to be sick, it should've been me. My daughter graduated from high school in 2017 and went to the National Guard. Also in 2017, his wife was diagnosed with an aggressive illness, I wondered if the stress of my relationship with her husband over the years caused her sickness. Unfortunately, she passed away in October 2017. My daughter's father had been married to her for almost 50 years by that time. Honestly, I thought I'd pass before either of them did. Everyone was devastated by her passing. I remember telling God that it should've been me. She forgave me to such a degree that there was no tension between us. I could drop my daughter off at their house without any drama. I could talk to her and her children and there were no elephants in the room. It is one thing to know and believe in the forgiveness of sin through Christ Jesus, knowing what He did for me and it's another level to see someone walk in that level of forgiveness and that was Annie Ruth Talbert.

One of the most glorious parts of being in Christ is learning to forgive others. When I think of Jesus hanging on the cross for my sins with all power to remove Himself and come down from the cross, knowing that He could have "passed the cup from Himself" and yet He endured the cross, the scourging, being spat upon and ridiculed and ultimately dying in my place... His wife had every just cause to hate me, but she didn't, instead, she showed me more grace and love than I ever deserved. It was easier to forgive others than it was to forgive myself. Today I try to live a life of gentleness and forgiveness.

I didn't deserve to be forgiven. I have no room to hold anything over the heads of anyone. When you walk in forgiveness, it's a glorious thing. Even if those family members who harmed me never come to me and apologize, they don't have to because they're already forgiven. I don't even care anymore. I want them to come to the Lord for themselves, not for me. God never works on the other person. He works on you first. Others must come to that place of surrendering to God on their own.

I never thought I would get married, in fact, I had resigned myself to being single for the rest of my life and I was okay with that. So two years after his wife passed away my daughter's father and I started talking, which wasn't unusual because although we had severed the intimate part of our relationship for well over 10 years, we still maintained a friendship. It started with a phone call. I don't know who called who, but it was first conversations then dinner and movies.

We married in 2019. It wasn't something we planned or something that I even considered after his wife passed. I remember him saying I was the only person he wanted to talk to. He knew me. I knew his children and grandchildren. We had history. We have a daughter. I didn't jump at the chance. Instead, I prayed about it. After I agreed, we went to marital counseling, and although I knew the Word, I wanted to make sure it was okay to get married. The Bible says if the husband dies, the wife is no longer bound to the husband due to his passing. That's the only reason I had the liberty and freedom to marry and be at peace with him. He never abandoned his wife, he stayed with her long before she ever became ill and remained with her wife until she passed. And I'm so happy about that.

A few family members struggled with the idea of us getting married and I completely understood, but they came around and have come to love him even more. It was hard, even my daughter had difficulty accepting the marriage. She felt like we were waiting for Na'na to die. When I heard her concerns, I had to check myself. Was I waiting? I had to ask myself some hard questions. And the answer was a definitive 'no.' I had moved on in my heart. I wasn't salivating and waiting to take my chance. I had been single for so long after things ended between us. I was experiencing life on my terms. I'd once gone to **"Singles Night"** at my church with my sister and men weren't approaching us. I went on a date with someone I was in ministry with. I thought things might've turned out well, but nothing came of it. I had a conversation with my pastor during our marriage counseling and told him I didn't understand why I was still single. It didn't have anything to do with weight, color or size. I remember my pastor said, "You just happen to be single" at this time. I have no regrets about marrying my husband.

My husband is very guarded about the subject of our marriage. He knows everyone that I do life with. I don't get a lot of static from his family or friends. If anyone feels a certain way about us being married, I don't know about it. I'm not a person that likes to intrude and I've developed that based on the rejection I experienced as a child. If someone has a problem with me, I won't be in their presence long.

Even during the affair, I never had a moment of peace, I was tormented more than I was in love. No one ever gets away with sin. The scriptures are very clear. By the time I came to God, my life was a complete wreck. From molestation, an addiction to pornography, abortions and sexual affairs, all before I was twenty-five years old, and at that time I didn't know what a wreck I was making of my life.

At the time of the affair, I was deeply attached to him but as I came to know Jesus more and more, I realized I could not do both and I had to let him go and hang on to Jesus, Christ was pulling me to Himself and it is only in Christ that I have found what real love, unfailing love looks like. It's in the cross of Christ.

19 For just as through one man's disobedience the many
were made sinners, so also through the one man's obedience
the many will be made righteous. 20 The law came along
to multiply the trespass. But where sin multiplied, grace

multiplied even more 21 so that, just as sin reigned in death, so also grace will reign through righteousness, resulting in eternal life through Jesus Christ our Lord.
Romans 5:19-21

Jesus paid the price for sin, so we don't have to however there are consequences to sin… and God's grace is sufficient even in those consequences.

One day, I was looking in the mirror, overwhelmed with guilt and shame for everything I'd done. I asked God, why did you save me? He said, "I knew the person you would become." His love and forgiveness are amazing. Sexual sin is one of the most difficult sins to live in and walk out of because it's to the body, which encompasses the soul, mind, and spirit, and there's a constant battle in the mind of the sin.

I always loved the arts; God has used me to write and direct many plays all pertaining to the saving grace of Jesus Christ. It's my way of showing and telling the stories of redemption, I have compassion for people who are in bondage to sexual sin but with that, I also carry the solution which is only found in Christ. The hope of glory. It doesn't matter what the sexual bondage is, if it goes against God's word and it grieves and tortures you and you desire to get out, I want you to know Jesus came to set the captives free and you can be free in Christ. It's important to come to know who Christ is. There is an eternity and God will judge us for our sins. It's a sure thing. It doesn't matter what the sin is; God's love has the power to overshadow the sins and the hurts. Whatever the hurt is, let it hurt. God can and will heal. There was a song that came out many years ago by Anthony Brown titled "Worth". This is the amazing love of Jesus. Because I was not worth saving, my sins were many, a thief, fornicator, adulterer, and murderer… too many to count but in His mercy and grace He saved me, and when viewed from this place of humility I can see what Christ has done and continually doing in me. He's worthy of all the praise and glory, I'm only here because of Him. He's kind and merciful to us and is waiting and wanting us to walk in victory. It's time to walk in victory!

"Placing God first, submitting to his will, and having an encouraging and supportive sisterhood helped me heal."

Victory in Seeking God First

TIFFANY COLEMAN

I remember being a child and wondering what my purpose was in this world. As a young girl I remember thinking about my life as an adult. I knew that I wanted to be married with kids and I knew that I wanted to work in a professional environment. I did not really consider what type of professional career I would have, but I was certain that it would require that I wear heels every day. As the oldest of my two sisters, I had the most responsibility. As a child, I did not understand and sometimes resented what at the time felt unfair and I longed to escape. After all, I was a child. I just wanted to dance like Janet Jackson and participate in extracurricular activities, not look after my sisters, and do chores. When I reached adulthood, I began to appreciate my mom for the responsibilities she had given me as it prepared me for life.

My mother had four children. My brother and I are from her first marriage and my two sisters from her second. I was three years old when my mother remarried, and my brother was six. My brother never lived with us, he lived with our great aunt and uncle, but would visit some weekends. Mom said it was not intentional, however, when my mother went into labor with me, my brother stayed with her aunt and uncle and the rest is history. My mother's husband adopted me at seven years of age. Funny, how I still remember that day…vaguely but I remember. I wondered why my biological father allowed this, why he did not want me. My brother would see him when he came into town. I can even remember times when he picked my brother up for the weekend. Sometimes my brother and I would talk about it, and he would tell me all about dad and say, "dad loves you; he's just waiting for you to grow up".

My dad and I began to talk and occasionally spend time together when I entered high school. Although I was being raised by my moms' husband and carried his name, I longed for a relationship with my biological father. I was so excited to finally get to know the man that I had only known through my brother. We bonded and agreed that I would move to Florida and live with him after graduating high school to become better acquainted while I attended college. My senior year came, and I remember being so excited! I was finally about to finish high school. Suddenly the calls stopped coming, and the number was disconnected. I graduated high school, but dad was no longer in the plan.

I entered college in the fall of 1992. I still had not decided exactly what career I wanted to pursue beyond being a professional. I assumed that I would figure it out and I would be on campus with my off and on boyfriend of three years at the time. Consumed with relationship drama, I did poorly in college and after a year decided to take a breather. It wasn't until he and I married and became parents to my first-born daughter, Bria Christina did I really become serious about my future. I was only twenty years old and now responsible for someone other than myself. A beautiful baby girl whose precious life was in my hands.

Becoming a mother was probably the first turning point in my life. It took me back to being a young girl and wondering what my purpose was in this world. Being young, a mother and married was not easy at all. I tried to imitate what I had seen growing up, but it was far too complicated. I did not know how to balance marital issues, mothering and securing my future. Most times I felt overwhelmed and frustrated. I did not understand why it was so complicated, I just knew that it was. We divorce when Bria was only two.

I found myself in a place of seeking. Who was I, what could I offer myself and this child? What is my purpose? I went to church, but I did not study the bible much for myself. My grandfather was a Baptist Pastor, a man that I held in high regard. He would tell me when he felt I was drifting, but he did it with such love and compassion. I adored him. He was a constant in my life. No matter what he was always there for me. I was his Tiffany Toooo. Although we were so close, I struggled with drawing close to God in the traditional Baptist setting. I mean, my grandfather was a wonderful man of God, but some church members were very judgmental and made me feel uncomfortable. The focus seemed to be more on looking and acting the part instead of showing love to save souls. I did not find pleasure in acting. After all, acting the part was the reason why I had already been married and divorced. I was taught that marriage was the right thing to do if you wanted to live as an adult, but I did not know that it would be so hard or how to deal with the continuous unnecessary challenges.

I began to visit other churches as I sought to find a place where I belong.

A place where I would not be judged or criticized, just welcomed, and loved. Somehow, I landed at Bethany. At that time there was only one location in Baker, LA. Bethany was inviting and uplifting, and I did not feel judged or criticized. I visited Bethany off and on for several years but had never participated in cell group to get acquainted with other members. Because of that, I always felt like a visitor. Around that time, I was also struggling with the fact that I was a single mother. That was never a part of the plan. Growing up, I knew that I wanted to be married and have children, not just have children. I began to feel isolated at Bethany because I had not established a community and I attended alone. I saw couples that appeared to be happy all around me and felt that having the right companion would complete my life. I would have a family again and this time we would worship together under a solid foundation. I told myself that my marriage did not work because my ex-husband was selfish, immature and he did not take marriage seriously. He was not ready to be a husband and father and there was nothing I could have done to change that.

I decided to start college again with a serious mindset. At this time, I was dating a guy that I knew but did not know as he visited my grandfather's church several times annually. I was told that he had inquired about me several times over the years. We dated a couple of years before he mentioned the idea of marriage. He said he did not care that I had married before, and although he had never been married, he ignored the fact that I had. I felt so grateful that this man had pursued and chosen me. Pleasing him was most important to me. He was educated, intelligent and stable. I put him above everything and loved him more than I loved myself. The first few years of the marriage were busy. I was a mother, wife, professional and student. I worked hard to succeed in each area. Many times I felt unappreciated and ignored but determined not to fail this time, I pressed hoping it would get better. I felt as if I was on a roller coaster, and he was the operator. After many years of this vicious cycle of difficulties, now having three kids, I walked away taking nothing but a sofa, my kids, and our clothes.

By this time I had earned a bachelor's degree in business management, but I did not have a thriving source of income at this time with three children to provide for. I was a self-employed cosmetologist before the unexpected pregnancy with my youngest daughter. We decided that I would stay home a while when she was born, and the split occurred before I could rebuild my business. I was an emotional wreck, but I had to be strong for my children. At times I did not know if I was coming or going. When the kids were away, I would lay in my dark, quiet apartment on my air mattress crying for hours. I started visiting Bethany again before leaving my husband and this time I joined a small group. These sisters, my mother, godmother, and several other dear friends from different phases of my life held me up in my season of brokenness. They walked the journey out with me, they blessed me, they encouraged me, and they believed in me when I did not believe in myself. They spoke life into me. They gave us food, furniture, electronics, linens, and money. We were flooded with blessings!

This was the beginning of a new season for me. Life changed drastically. It was swim or sink. My oldest daughter graduated a few months after the separation and started college, while my son was in his last year of middle school and baby girl was only two years of age. I worked three jobs for a season to make ends meet. It is funny how we did not have much but found joy in the simple things. Every Friday we would rent a couple of movies from red box and pick up a papa murphy's pizza and microwave popcorn. We had so much fun! Sometimes after church on Sundays my son would make waffles, and I would scramble eggs and cut up fruit for our brunch. If we had enough money, we would use our George Foreman grill to cook our pork chops. Looking back, I realize how great life was then. We did not have much, but we had each other and that is what really mattered.

Life was hard, but God was with me. Every month on paper it seemed as if I did not have enough to cover my expenses, but every month every bill was paid. The healing process took time, and I made mistakes along the way, but God never left me. He stayed right there and waited for me. Finally, I surrendered. I was tired of acting out of my hurt, living broken and lost. I never outwardly or verbally blamed God for my failed marriages, but my actions may have suggested that. After looking for love in all the wrong places. I decided to look for love in God. This was my awakening.

When I truly surrendered to God the healing began. In this season, I earned my master's degree in nonprofit administration and God's started revealing the raw, uncut version of Tiffany to me. Before now, I only saw what those who hurt me had done. I did not recognize where I messed up. Funny how we see everyone else's flaws but are completely oblivious to our own. We may not cause the issue, but our response or reaction to the issue can be just as bad. Not one time did I consult God before dating or marrying. I chose who I wanted on my own. Then after coming to the realization that we were unequally yoked I wanted God to fix it. When the load became heavy, I called on him, but did not understand the process to weather the storm. He revealed unresolved wounds of rejection, insignificance, feeling unloved, bitterness, insufficiency and exhaustion from battling verbal and mental abuse. The revelations were so profound, but not easy to overcome. I blamed myself for not protecting me and vowed that I would do so from this day forward. I could no longer be too passive, naïve, and trusting. After all, this always caused me way too much heartache. Reconciliation had taken place with my father, but total forgiveness had not at that point. I dealt with him cautiously without expectation. I was guarded. Even in divorce I felt like I had something to prove to my ex. I had to prove that I could survive without him, he did not break me, and that he could not control me. I was free yet still in bondage mentally. The prayers of my mother, godmother and fellowshipping with other woman who shared their testimonies of the trials God brought them through were a source of comfort during this time. Still the walls were up, and I determined that the old Tiffany had died and been buried, and new Tiffany would be in control from now on. I spent several years thinking that I could in and of myself establish a wall of protection from pain and disappointment. Boy was I wrong! The enemy has a way of allowing us to think we are in control. That is farthest from the truth. Things began to spiral, and I realized that I had become what I complained about when describing some Baptist church members. I was playing the role, but not living it. One night after really looking in the mirror, I determined that enough was enough. Something had to change.

By this time, my second child Tyler Benjamin had started college. Baby girl, Loryn Tiffani was the product of shared custody. On the weeks I did not have her, I would come home from work, shower, and meditate in the presence of God until falling asleep. I had experienced so much pain that I no longer trusted myself to make relationship decisions. Seemingly successful, or at least productive in every area of my life but that. I cried out to God and repented for not seeking him until now. I had to accept accountability for my actions. I made several informed decisions without him and in return I suffered the consequences. Looking in the mirror was tough, yet necessary. It was at this time I came to the realization that God was the love I had been searching for. He was everything that I needed, and his words were the instructions I had been looking for. He was my provided, my example, my way maker, my strong tower, my burden bearer, my priest, and my protector. I determined that if it were God's will for me to be in a dating relationship, he would send someone that loved him and was serious about honoring him, someone ready to be my husband and I would be ready to be his wife. If it was not his will, I would serve and honor him and be content.

I always heard the saying "God's timing is not our timing." I am sure that I have said it a time or two myself. Life was beginning to feel complete. God was in his rightful place. Two kids in college and baby girl halfway through elementary school. Dad and I had truly reconciled and grown close. I purchased my own home, vehicle, and my professional life was developing.

All is well and I was in a peaceful place. Walking down the hallway of my organization in my heels one day I notice this man in a blue uniform looking at me. My immediate reaction was to ignore him. My mindset was "I have surrendered to God, and I am not getting caught up again. This is the enemy trying to take me out!" Lol, but seriously. A couple of days later, a young lady who worked at the same organization asked if I was in a relationship and mentioned that she knew a nice man that expressed interest in me. Standing firm to my decision to let God be my guide, I explained that I was not interested. She listened intently and nodded with understanding, then she said, just check out his Facebook page, you might change your mind. She told me his name and I agreed to check out his page not really intending to but did so to end the conversation.

I remember going home that evening and spending time with God, as it had become a part of my routine. Amid my quiet time, I remembered the conversation I had with the young lady at work. I went back and forth in my head for a while, trying to ignore the voice saying look at his Facebook page. Ok...I conceded and looked him up on Facebook determined to find every flaw I could possibly find. Never had I searched someone's Facebook page with such intention before. It was crazy! By the end of the week, I had searched every nook and cranny of his page at least four times. I found nothing that I could hold against him. He crossed my path several times that week while at work and always spoke with a big infectious smile. I would speak and keep it moving! I decided to talk to God about him but feared that it was another trap. Weeks later, I met a close girlfriend for dinner. We discussed the current events of my life, Loryn Tiffani, who she godmothered, then I mentioned Lorenzo. She asked me if I was going to get to know him and I told her no and that I was afraid. She asked had I prayed about it. I said yes and explained my concerns. She heard me out and then she explained that the spirit of fear was not from God. She continued by saying you say you have sought God for forgiveness, healing, and restoration. Follow his lead. Surrender your past to him COMPLETELY!!! Then she asked to see a picture of him and responded "Girl that is a good-looking fine man right there! You can let God give away your blessing if you want nah!"

Lorenzo and I exchanged numbers and began texting. After a couple of days, he called, and we started having text and phone conversations. I attentively observed his conversation for inconsistency or any signs of bad character but did not find anything other than he worked a lot and often ate chicken noodle soup after long days of work. I prayed relentlessly for God to show me if I should entertain conversation and told him that I was fine with us talking but that I was not interested in dating. He later admitted that he was initially bothered by my bold declaration before having a full conversation. However, he accepted that at least I was open to being his friend, so he went along with that. Weeks passed and we continued to talk a few times a week but that was the extent of it. The holiday season arrived, and my cousin convinced me to contact him to ask if he wanted to meet us to listen to a band. I did reluctantly and he came. Seeing him out of uniform was different. I saw him in a new light. We all talked and enjoyed the band. I was pleased by the fact that his eyes did not seem to roam. He seemed attentive and safe. We continued to talk, and he offered two opportunities for me to consider going on a date with him. After all, I had invited him to listen to live music with my cousin and I so perhaps I was having a change of heart. We ended up going on both dates and we have been together ever since!

Lorenzo was the perfect gentleman and my mom approved of him. He always walked me to the passenger side of the vehicle to open the door for me. He shifted his work schedule to spend more time with me, he was an open book, willing to address any concerns; but most of all, I loved the fact that he was consistent and comfortable being vulnerable. We dated only six months before marrying. He made it clear early on that he was dating with intentions. He shared that he had been married twice previously and dated since, but that he could not seem to find the one. I remember praying to God and asking him to send me someone who had traveled a similar path as I had. Someone who could relate to my past and understand instead of judging or feeling that they were above me. We had both experienced pain and relationship failure, been adopted by our mothers' husbands, and parented three children. I was like... ok God!

I had never met a man so intentional. Although I prayed that if it were God's will, he would send me someone who was ready to be my husband and loved him primarily, I still questioned. I still struggled from my past and fear plagued me. We talked about God, worshipped together, shared messages and gospel songs. He was humble, transparent, and respectful. He told me that he understood my fear and he would show me that he was sincere. Our children embraced each other and blended well for the most part. I mean to me they get along like biological siblings. Occasional sibling rivalry as everyone adjusted but nothing too serious. We started intense pre-marital counseling and planned a wedding to take place five weeks after our final session. Our counselor was no nonsense! He did not play with us and held us accountable to the word of God. I appreciate Pastor Harry for that. We currently attend the church that he pastors.

After marrying, our plan was to wait a couple of years before purchasing a house together. We determined that we would live in my home since Lorenzo lived in an apartment. We would look at house listings just to determine what type of house we would want when we were ready to purchase. One day we decided to schedule a tour of a house on one of the listings just because we thought the exterior was unique. We loved the house and decided that if we qualified (we were not prequalified) we would make an offer. Within twenty-four hours we made an offer, and our offer was accepted. Three days later, we put my house on the market and the next day the first viewer made an offer. Tell me what God will not do!

I was happy and sad. My house was a symbol of my accomplishment. It was purchased with God's help alone. That was the place where I surrendered to God and truly made him first and foremost. The place that I died and was born again in him. Now I was preparing to leave my place and move into ours. The new home was larger, and in the area I aspired to move to. I was pleased with all of that, but as I thought about letting go of the home that I found comfort in, the enemy of fear came again. The last days there were tearful, but I moved on to our beginning. I realize that too many times I allowed fear to hold me captive and hinder me. 2 Timothy 1:7 says for God has not given us the spirit of fear, but power and of love and a sound mind. I remind myself of that daily, as I am aware of how much power I have unknowingly given fear in my life. God's love, healing and restoration is so much bigger than fear. I have learned to take authority over the enemy and stand on God's word. I have learned to seek him FIRST in all things. I have learned to put no one or nothing before him. I still face trials and tribulation, but I am confident that in every situation God will work it out for my good and I surround myself with individuals that remind me of God's word and his faithfulness. For a long time, I wondered what my purpose was on this earth and why it had to be so hard. Walking out God's plan may not be easy but the fruit of striving to stay on course is so rewarding. Now I know that my purpose in life is to share my story and encourage you to seek God. He should be your first love.

In this life, we will have ups and downs. We will make mistakes. It is important to forgive ourselves for our mistakes. There were many times when I felt embarrassed about my failed marriages and wanted to hide in shame. I have also had moments when I succumbed to being the victim, but I had to check myself. I recognized where I went wrong. There were some red flags that I ignored. Forgiving other people was easier than forgiving myself. I did not trust myself to make good decisions when it came to dating and was hesitant to give my husband a chance because of that. I finally have victory because I learned to trust God and know who I am in him. I know my worth and what I deserve as a child of the King. God orders my steps and directs my path.

All of us have different stories and have traveled different paths. I have had some ups and downs. I have been through divorce and was not sure that real love would ever find me. God healed me in my singleness. He drew me closer to Him and allowed me to feel his love first, then sent my true love. We have been married for over three years now with a beautiful, blended family of six children and four grandchildren.

It is okay to fall as long as you get back up. Consult God about ALL things and trust him to guide your path. God showed up and showed out in my life when I surrendered completely. I am still a work in progress but a living witness that God can take a broken vessel and restore to newness greater than before.

"If you want something different, you will have to do the work to make the change. But nothing changes if nothing changes."

The Victorious Journey

LISA COLLINS

*S*elf-interest is not a state of selfishness. I would prioritize others before myself, which is not uncommon for women, particularly for women of color, but now my priority is selfcare. I define my journey of self-care as my steps to emotional, spiritual, and physical well-being. My journey begins with the story of the winter in 1999 and I share my reflections of this journey with you.

In the winter of 1999, I had just moved from Las Vegas, Nevada back to my hometown of St. Louis, Missouri. One night at a local wine bar, I met a man who would later become my husband and my daughter's father. This was to be a new phase in my life where my identity became significant other, mother, wife….a time of many joys, challenges, and a loss of self-prioritization.

Winter of 2023 is approaching as I capture reflections of my life on paper, there have been many seasons of changes… A lot has changed.

My daughter came into this world in November 2000. In September of 2003, our family of three relocated to New Orleans, Louisiana for a new job opportunity. I married the father of my daughter in August 2005. I became mother and wife with a career. Life was good, but seasons change and with change came more struggles, challenges, and celebrations. In April 2016, my position with the company in New Orleans was eliminated. The loss of that position was the first step of my journey to self-care. As a partner of the financial security for my family, I needed to secure income. Although my initial focus was supporting my family, in September 2016, believing in myself and my ability to succeed, I formed my own company, Collins Accounting Services

Group, LLC. Despite seasons of growing pains, my small business is 100% female and successful.

My life was embracing new seasons of more change, challenges, growth, and opportunities. I took a long look back at the start of my journey in 1999 and realized I was no longer the same person, the wife, mother, and caretaker of everyone else. Over the years I had developed self-interest, exploring things that would fulfill my needs. My daughter, no longer a child, had completed her undergraduate degree in May 2022. She has a wonderful job, a great friend group, and lives an independent life. I'm very proud of her! My self-realization also identified a major change in my relationship with my spouse and in August 2022, our divorce was finalized.

The details of my journey are not important, but the lessons learned have been life changing. I would like to share some of those lessons. This list is not in order of importance. They are all part of my belief system.

1. **Self-interest is not selfish.** I would prioritize the needs of others over my own needs. No one made me do it. I always thought I was doing the right thing if someone needed me. Or, needed something from me. I didn't realize how much of myself I was giving. Not until I started getting mad about it. *I now understand it's ok to decline an opportunity to give of oneself.* And, you don't owe anyone an explanation.

2. **Don't make agreements you can't keep.** It's just added pressure and stress on yourself. You just end up twisting yourself into a pretzel and most likely taking it out on the person you made the agreement with. Just use the words *"I don't want to make an agreement with you that I can't keep".*

3. **Communicate, Communicate, Communicate.** If you feel turbulence, address it. Discuss the elephant in the room. This was a hard one for me. I learned to address the issue instead of pointing and blaming. Instead of starting with *"I don't like it when you…"* Try *"I don't have a good experience when (insert your own statement) happens.*

4. **Don't be afraid to change the nature of your relationships**. People change, priorities shift, life happens. Addressing these changes can enhance your relationships. Relationships don't have to end. They can get better.

5. **Understand the level of hurt.** Is it a paper cut? A stab wound? Or something bigger. *Do the work to heal.* It's for you. Resist the compulsion to bring up the hurt with the person involved unless it's a part of the healing process. However, you may sometimes have to let the person know you're still hurting. Instead of bring up the entire event try saying *"I'm still healing."* Or *"I haven't healed yet."* Let that statement hang in the air.

6. **Work with a Therapist.** Working with an independent, unbiased, unrelated professional was one of the best decisions I made. I worked with a therapist for almost a year before I let my ex know I wanted a divorce. I was more concerned about his feelings than mine. My therapist helped me with this. After finally letting my ex know I wanted a divorce, we worked on me for the next year.

While working on myself I told the universe that I would be open to dating. The universe responded. A wonderful man that also did the work on himself came into my life. We share elements of the same belief system. We don't need each other. We want to be together. He spends part of his time in Africa working on a project closely aligned to his belief system. I've structured my company where I can work from any location with reliable internet service. I have run my company from Africa. I made adjustments to my work hours due to the time difference. So far it has been a great experience.

We know ourselves better than anybody. I am not encouraging anyone to leave their partner, but I am encouraging you to choose your happiness. It's important to believe in yourself. It's okay to be afraid, but it's not okay not to try. If you want something different, you will have to do the work to make the change. But nothing changes if nothing changes. We all deserve happiness, but it's up to us to create it for ourselves. Don't allow the low moments of your life to determine how you live your life moving forward. Take your life back and live the victorious life you deserve!

"Before I ever knew what an enemy was, I had one."

Victory Over My Enemy

DANIELLE ANDERSON

The most challenging thing that I've ever had to do in my life was to keep breathing... after taking that first breath from my mother's womb. When I came into this world, whether I was ready or not, the battle was on its way. My family had been chosen to fight against a strong enemy - one that would strip you of power and cause you to believe you're weak. One that would chain you up in all of your thoughts, actions, and emotions. One that would sabotage your family and shatter the system meant to protect you. He knew how to leave you gasping for air. This enemy knew how to make you scream for help and cause you to feel that every ear around you had been stricken with some affliction of muteness. He knew how to launch a death grip that could leave you crippled and paralyzed... the grip that would devour all that I could've ever imagined becoming. I was so young when life would begin to prove itself unfair. I didn't know what I had inside of me, but my response to what was ahead would be proven to me and everyone watching, just what I was made of.

What I didn't know is we needed help, an ally. It would only require One to win this battle. I'd heard about Jesus, but how do you solicit a General like that? Back then, I didn't know Him like I do now. I didn't know of His mighty power or His infinite wisdom. I had never experienced His strategic abilities to attack and defeat every single foe. I didn't know of His great love for me and my family or how even when it seemed that I was losing, I was truly winning. And I most certainly did not understand the simplicity of having a relationship with Him. I learned that every trial helped me to discover another part of God's faithfulness and loving kindness to me.

My Dad's name is Wilbert Coats Jr., but most people knew him by Paco. Daddy was so cute and such a stud. He had deep dimples with the most beautiful smile you'd every seen before. He had salt and pepper hair that would find its way to him by the time he reached middle school. It depends on who tells the story, but if you listen to his account, the girls loved it. He had the "bad boy" streak in him that secretly every girl liked - even the good ones. His walk emitted a bold, I'm not afraid of anything, type of stance. He was pure man strength, and confidence. Daddy was cocky, and he had no problem standing up for us or anyone else if he needed to. He wasn't passive or afraid to confront the misdirections that we had in life. If we were wrong, he spoke up and graciously handed out the consequences that would follow. Sometimes, I would rather receive the punishment instead of his hours-long conversation about why what we did was wrong. Daddy knew how to be gentle and affectionate. He was playful and had the most corny jokes that I would laugh and cry about, mostly because I just loved him. His favorite saying became, "Don't do like I do, do like I say do." That's because he knew *his* example wasn't suitable to raise the kind of kids he desired us to be.

My Mom's name is Christy Sims. She was tall and beautiful. She was a lean, and sassy woman. Everyone called her *Christy Love*. Over the years, the name would become a term of affection expressed by all who knew her. Mama was the one who would speak her mind and maybe even give you a few choice words. Somehow people respected her even more and would always end up returning to the comfort of her company. She was absolutely loveable and something about her would captivate every person that she met. From cousins, to friends in school, to complete strangers, something about mama's character would suck people right in. Daddy didn't have eyes big enough for her. He loved her more than anything in this world and everyone knew it.

My dad was a very educated man and could articulate himself in the most beautiful ways. He had the ability to convince people that he was right even if he knew he was dead wrong. He wasn't afraid to ask people for help or acknowledge his shortcomings. My mom was a little on the hood side and she owned every bit of it. She was the one carrying a stick walking up to you saying, *Oh, I wish you would… run up on me, I'ma show you…* There was one time a girl in the neighborhood who was much older than my sister begin to bother her.

Mama got a bat, went to the girl's house and dared her or her mama to come outside. They both ran back in and locked the door. She was tall and lean, but she had the courage of a lion. There was no kind of graceful articulation in her vocabulary. Some of it, I can't write in this book! But to me, it made her all the more beautiful. She stayed true to who she was. Our friends loved her so much. She was so cool. My cousins called her their favorite auntie, and many people have stories that Mama was closer to them than their own mother. She was so relatable and would make you feel at ease in her company. Many things would happen to Mama that clawed at her life, like the paws of a lion tearing a strong bull into pieces. Mama would tell us stories of her being whipped with an extension cord, or feelings of being the least favorite child. My mom didn't know her dad like she'd hoped to and sometimes that alone can take a toll on you. After she met my dad, eventually this relationship would lead to more disappointments and insecurities for mama.

Sometimes it's good not to know or understand everything when you're young, because when you do, it can cause you to give all the way up. I didn't realize it then, but I would soon come to learn that my life would leave me feeling like a pillow had been placed over my face with the sole purpose of destroying me before I had the chance to really live. Sometimes it felt as if I didn't have the opportunity to try or fail. All of my efforts would be mocked by attempts without any completions and would eventually push me into my comfort zone… insecurity and repetitive failure.

Before I ever knew what an enemy was, I had one. He would kill my identity before I had the chance to discover who I was. The enemy would destroy any belief I had in myself to dream or hope and would challenge who and what I believed in. I would ultimately be chained in ways that would leave me bound and helpless. My thoughts were not my own, I thought what he told me to think. I had no clue of who I was. I walked in rejection and eventually carried the shame of my parents. This is what I put on each and everyday. Looking back, I realized something kept my heart from the temptation of becoming hard and cold. Even though it would be broken countless times and even more again, it could never stop loving. That was Jesus. He gave me a heart like His. And no matter how broken your heart is right in this moment, He has given you a heart like His as well. Just ask Him to take it away. All of the hurt and all of the pain

45

and all of the disappointments. It's as simple as that. Now you may have to pray this for a season until your heart becomes free, but the prayer doesn't need to be complicated. Having a forgiving heart was a blessing to me because there were so many other places in me that were broken - wasting away. When I received love, I gave love. When I received rejection, I gave love. When I was misused, I gave love, and when the love stopped - I still gave love. Forgiveness would be a source of ammunition for what would come.

"You're blessed when you feel you've lost what is most dear to you. Only then can you be embraced by the One most dear to you."
Matt. 5:4 MSG

Within the first few years of life, I lived carefree, happy, adventurous, shy, and always smiling. Sometime around the age of 7, I realized I wasn't the sparkle in Daddy's eye as much as I would've liked to be, and neither were my siblings - Damon and Nicole. At the time, I was the youngest of the three of us and ten years later would come the twins, Dekeeta and Deveeta. But not being Daddy's prize began to unravel me in ways that could not be understood. The embracing of it came with time; it takes supernatural help and humility to love someone that is unable to reciprocate it back to you. But that's how Christ loves us - unconditionally. Having the capacity to embrace the fact that you are not Daddy's girl would be the avenue to healing for me in depths I could've never imagined. And not just for me, Daddy, Mama, and my siblings.

The days, months, and years had gone by and Daddy sat me down and shared a hard truth with me. The translation of what Daddy told me was, "A thief has come in our home, his plan is to take every dream your Mom and I had for ourselves and for each of you. He will violate you and leave you with pains and scars that I can't help you recover from and some you may never recover from. And the hardest part for me is, I'm the one that allowed him to come in." Daddy stood up, gently kissed me on my forehead, and said, "Dani, I love you," as he walked away, hanging his head in shame and disappointment. Some part of me wanted to scream, "Da, it's okay, I'm not upset with, please just remember to never stop loving me!!..." But no words would part from my lips. I sat there dumbfounded asking God, why did he place me in a family like this? God, how could you allow me to feel this much pain? I'm only a kid! I was in Second Grade.

The best way he knew how, daddy had just told me that he was on drugs. He used the needle to shoot up. If that wasn't enough, I learned that mama was also using. DEVASTATION and BETRAYAL! All I could think was, why? I hate this family! I don't want to be here anymore! Now, I understood what had been taking daddy away from us all this time. I understood better why we didn't have a spoon available to eat cereal or stir cake batter, or maybe why the lights and water were off. It helped me to understand why I didn't have a towel to bathe with or why I had to use baking soda for toothpaste. Things became crystal clear.

Even while under the weight of what had been told to me, I did seem to remember Daddy say, "I love you, Dani." Sometimes, I had trouble believing it, but it was always something I longed to hear. God knows if it had been expressed in a more consistent and healthy way, my heart would've been unbound from the life sentence of rejection and shame that it would serve. I knew now, I was suffering from Daddy's choice to let the thief come in. This wasn't a thought in my head at the time, but after cooling my temper, the love I had for my father would completely overwhelm any hurt or disappointment. The response of my heart would now be, "You before me." I begin to live my life in this way for Mama and Daddy - and for my sisters and brother if necessary. Whatever I needed could wait for the sake of them.

The life I was now choosing to live was about to teach me what true sacrifice is and how to love like Jesus loved me. How to lay down my life for someone who most counted as undeserving. How to love when it's unfair. How to love when all the rules are broken. How to remain loyal and stand as a rod until the storm passed. The bond between my siblings and I strengthened like never before. We learned how to adjust and adapt and look out for one another. If it meant eating cereal with a fork, we did it without complaining. If it meant having to burn candles because the lights were turned off, we did it. If it meant changing the twins diapers and feeding them, we did it. If it meant tending to mama's black eye, we did it. If it meant loving them over and over and over again, we did it. This way of living became the norm for us. In a season where it was reasonable to think we would be served by our parents, we humbly learned to serve them. And looking back, I don't think any of us would change one moment of it. I count it an honor. We learned that even when it rains, the sun will shine again.

Life kept going, and I kept growing up. I was in school, and my siblings and I were always involved in literacy camps over the summer and other activities that were offered in school and the community. My dad's family always stepped in to provide opportunities that kids in our situation may have not been able to do. I loved it, but I had no dreams of my own. I lived each day with no sense of purpose. As I became an adult and had children of my own, someone very dear to me whose name was Pamela Gauthier once told me, "If your kids are unable to figure out their purpose, it's your responsibility to give them one!" I needed someone to help me figure out the point of my existence. Many days of my life I felt insignificant - a disappointment to many. Everyone would always say I had the prettiest smile, and I did, just like daddy. However, no one knew the pain hidden behind that smile. There was so much pain and turmoil inside of me that I didn't know how to navigate, and there was no one around who dared to ask me the question that I longed to hear: *Are you okay?* I understand its such a heavy question to ask, because it takes discipline, grace and determination to walk life out with people and be able to give them wisdom and not your opinions, just to fill the empty spaces. You got to be willing to seek the counsel of God's word. That's hard work and I'm sure that's why people don't ask that question. It takes a certain level of maturity and selflessness to get in the trenches with people to ensure victory for them.

For the majority of middle and high school, I fit in with the crowds. Our fun would consist of throwing eggs at people's homes, going to football games and dances, and cutting school to go to McDonald's to hang out. By this time, my home had been out of control for some years with my parents drug and alcohol usage. We would have precious nights of sleep interrupted by mama and daddy screaming and yelling in the middle of the night. One of the most horrifying nights of them all, was to wake up and realize that a stranger has come into our home in the middle of the night. I helplessly watched him tie mama's hands to the bed as he placed a knife to her throat and angrily told me to leave the room - I can't remember where daddy was, but I remember he wasn't there. What is he doing to my mom? I laid in the bed silently, helplessly, as the tears rolled down my face. Why is he hurting her? She doesn't deserve this! Everything had begin to take a toll on me and I started living life from this pain. I remember feeling rejected and unloved - helpless and stuck and afraid. I was insecure and dealt with feeling like I was always the odd person - a misfit. No one said that to me, but I just didn't feel comfortable being myself. My father was slowly missing the opportunity to help me understand my purpose or my value. I didn't feel valuable to him (although I was), and because of that, I had a hard time feeling valuable to anyone else. Subsequently, I began to fill the voids. I began dating, hanging out at parties with friends and life slowly but surely begin to really speed up. When I was fourteen I begin to secretly watch dirty movies and try to imitate what I would see the actors do. It just didn't feel right, so I stopped and moved on to the next thing...

By the age of sixteen, I did something that I would really regret. I lost my virginity, and I remember feeling like, I did all this sneaking and lying for this? History Class was way more exciting! Amongst friends, I pretended that I was excited and thrilled, but really it ended up being the open door to a really dark path for me. The bible says, "be sure, your sins will find you out." It wasn't long before my grandmother MaDear would say something to me just to let me know, that she know, what I was up to. It's amazing how your innocence can fall from under you in one selfish act. Sin is a stench on our life that can only be exposed to us by the Holiness of God. You will always deny your sin or even be oblivious to it until you let the Holy Conviction of Jesus into your life. How do we do that? SURRENDER NOW, while there's still time. I lost the glow on my face - the glow of purity and my innocence... I begin going to clubs and dressing in ways that showed the lack of respect that I had for myself. I was so lost, trying to find ways to numb the pain that I faced at home, but I was headed in a downward spiral and fast. *I had a father wound.* You may be wondering why so much of the responsibility is placed on my dad. It's because I innately counted on him to be the protector of our family. My story may sound contradictory in some ways when you hear that my dad was affectionate and somewhere else you may read I felt rejected by him. The answer to this is, in some ways you have to have lived this story in order to understand my point of view. I had to allow the wheat and the thistles grow together as Matthew 13 speaks of.

Daddy would say, "If people love you, they should show you because love is an action word." He was not the best example at times, and it cost me dearly. The older and more mature I got, I learned not to blame my dad. I understand so much better now that people can only give from what they've got. As a kid, I simply didn't have the capacity to see it that way. My dad and mom loved me with all that they had, and turns out, that was enough. But life got rough for me. While in college at the age of 19, I became pregnant. I told Mama because she was the most reasonable parent. The first thing she said was, either get rid of that baby or tell your daddy." I thought if I tell Daddy, me and the baby will die. My dad would be angry with me and most of all - disappointed. He had no patience for this kind of behavior and deep down I wanted to avoid anything else that would tear at our relationship, so I decided to do as mama told me and go to the local abortion clinic. I got there, and people were outside pleading with those of us who were going in. They were praying and had poster signs with words written on them. I remember that they were not rude or critical, but I tried to drown them out and at least get in the door without being a chicken. It was so scary. I entered the building and the place was so creepy, dark and depressing. The lady called me up, got my information and told me to have a seat. After waiting a while, they called me up behind the desk. She said a whole bunch of words, but the one's I heard clearly was, "ma'am, you are 3 months pregnant, and your baby has a heartbeat." *This takes my breath just writing about this.* I said, "Okay, and I took the appointment card and walked out of the office. *Lord, please don't let these ladies be out here and please forgive me for what I'm about to do. I just need to get this done and I'm gonna change my life...*

My best friend and I would laugh and cry so much together. I could share anything with her a she would listen and never become judgmental. She was always supportive, and always there for me, but it still wasn't enough to silence the voices I heard inside my head. I began contemplating suicide over and over and over again. I was convinced that if I killed myself, I would then get the love that I deserved. I went to the store, bought the bottle of pills and decided to take them. I decided I would take 20 pills before going to bed. I figured I could just pass away in my sleep and not have to do something that was painful. The thoughts of suicide increased day by day. No matter how much I tried, I could not escape the thoughts that had plagued the seven year old little girl. I set the day that I would go ahead and take myself out. *"Ma'am, your baby has a heartbeat."* The courage that was there diminished abruptly! I lost all heart and chickened out. The more I slept around, the more dirty and ragged and used I felt. I felt so alone even though people were always around. The little girl inside of me still longed for someone to ask, *"Are you okay?"* I felt so much shame, and I felt like everyone around me could see the dirtiness of my life. I felt absolutely worthless and that nothing in my life could be reconciled. By this time, I was an emotional wreck and completely chained to sexual sin. It had become a stronghold. I hated it. The goal had always been to be loved back, but instead, I felt like all life had been sucked out of me, and only my corpse remained. I had been used in such a way that would sink me into a deep, dark hole. Pain on top of pain, on top of pain. *God please help me?*

You're blessed when you're at the end of your rope. With less of you there is more of God and his rule.
Matt. 5:3 (MSG)

My heart still longed for true love to show up. At some point around my early twenties, I remember considering my salvation and wondering if I was right with Jesus. One thing Christy and Paco got right was making us attend church every Sunday. For most of my life I went because I was made to go, but all of a sudden, the words that the pastor would preach would begin to get my attention. My surrender to God, was birthed out of my desperation for Him. I was absolutely fed up with myself and the only choice left was the Lord. I was afraid that I would die in my sins and live without Jesus. Plainly put, I was scared to go to hell. I didn't have a prayer life or even knew what that was, but I remember asking, *"Lord, can you help me to hate what you hate and love what you love?"* And little by little, I begin to see my desires change. The relationship I was in at the time was a snare. My feet were tangled and bound, and I just couldn't break free on my own. That's how you know when something is a stronghold... you can't walk away from it, no matter how hard you try. You need the help of Jesus and a mama like his - Mrs. Donna. She said, "I want you to be free Danielle and I don't want you to go to hell for my son and nobody else. Jesus will set you free!" She prayed with me then and she still continues to pray for me til this day.

I felt so unworthy before God, but I knew I needed to look in the mirror and deal with what I'd been trying to avoid - Me. It took courage to admit to what I had become. I said one of those desperate prayers... *Lord, if you get me out of this, I won't mess up again.* Surely, I would mess up again. Thankfully, He knows us better than we know ourselves

Over time, God began to do everything I prayed for. I would like to interject that in my life there have been prayers that God did not answer for me, but my duty and honor shall always be to count Him faithful, because He is. It's not based on God's response to my prayer, it's based on who He says He is. God dissolved the emotionally controlled relationship for one. That was very painful and took years of healing for me. You must redefine the standards that God has given in your own life. Sex is reserved for your spouse - end of story; you were never meant to indulge in sex with anyone other than that. In marriage, the vow says, "The two shall become one." When engaging in this type of act with someone who is not your spouse, the two will *still* become one. That's why there's so much difficulty and pain after the breakup because God has to separate what had illegally become one.

As I began to search for the Lord wholeheartedly, He began to restore my value and self-worth, but it was only the beginning. During the season of asking God to cause me to hate what He hates, I also began to desperately cry out to Him. One night I turned on Juanita Bynum's *Behind the Veil* CD, I pleaded to the Lord to have mercy on me and to take away the guilt. I got on the floor in my little apartment, and I started praying a simple prayer. "Please help me, Lord. I don't want to go to hell. Save my soul, Lord. Forgive me Lord." As I prayed, something began to happen. I believe the devil realized that the Great General had been summoned, and his time was short. The Bible says in Ephesians 6:12, "For we wrestle not against flesh and blood, but against principalities, against powers, against the rulers of this world, against spiritual wickedness in high places." What I'm about to say, is not intended to scare you, but I have to share this because the Lord rescued my life in this way. As I listened to that CD and continued to pray, out of my mouth would come words, but they were not my own. They were from the devil. It was things like… *God hates you, you stinky whore.* That was something I'd heard daddy say to mama before. The devil began to mock me, saying *Nobody loves you. You are worthless.* Okay, so I began to get scared. I'm home alone and I don't know what in the world to do. But I continue to allow the CD to play because something is happening up in here.

I'd heard about demonic activity, but now this is happening, what seemed like in slow motion. After calling a friend from bible study group to inform her of what was happening to me, she immediately told me to come over. She started to pray for me and things were still being stirred up. After praying with her, I was set up to meet a dear couple, Mr. and Mrs. Lusk. God used them in the area of healing and deliverance. I went to her home with three ladies who were there to support me. They anointed my head with oil. I sit in that chair for three full hours, getting the devil cast out of me. The devil doesn't play fair. That's why the Bible teaches us to be careful about the places we go, the people we hang with, and the things we do and say. By this time, the devil had gained so much territory in my life. Mrs. Lusk commented that my soul was being carried behind me on a chain. I was out of it in a sense, but I was very aware when she asked someone, "Did this child's mother give her over to witchcraft or some type of cult?" The scene was heartbreaking and beautiful all at the same time. Healing and deliverance are God's love languages. The General had stepped in to save me. Now let me say this, you don't need to walk around in fear wondering if something like this is on your life. If it is, God will expose it, because as I stated earlier, He is faithful. And if something like this *is* on your life, He has the power to destroy it as he did for me.

I'd suffered so much over the years from the thief. The thief was Satan. He got in and wreaked havoc on both me and my family. After leaving the Lusk's home, I was traumatized. I felt afraid because I'd never seen or experienced anything like this before. I'd only heard about it. My body was weak and frail for weeks. I would just sit and tremble, needing to be refilled now by God's word. That night, when I got home, I didn't want to be alone. The ladies came back to my home to pray, but immediately when they walked in, they felt the Lord's presence. I was still scared. That was scarier to me than Jason, Michael, and Candyman combined! But the Lord would give me a scripture that night to confirm that He was with me and that I had no need to be afraid. I don't know if you've ever done this before, but I just flipped the bible open and said wherever it lands, Lord please encourage me. Psalm 18 is where the pages unfolded. I'll share a short piece, but read it if you get an opportunity.

"But me he caught — reached all the way from sky to sea; he pulled me out of that ocean of hate, the void in which I was drowning. They hit me when I was down, but God stuck by me. He stood me up on a wide-opened field; I stood there saved — surprised to be loved!

God made my life complete when I placed all the pieces before him. When I got my act together, he gave me a fresh start. Now I'm alert to God's ways; I don't take God for granted. I feel put back together, and I'm watching my step. God rewrote the text of my life when I opened the book of my heart to his eyes. Everyone who runs to him makes it.

When I chased my enemies I caught them; I nailed them down then I walked all over them. You armed me well for this fight. I ground them to dust; I threw them out, like garbage in the gutter. This God set things right for me and shut up the people who talk back. That's why I'm thanking you God, all over the world.

My life is forever indebted to the Lord. When I think of how He's forgiven the most shameful sins in my life. He's restoring my identity and making me complete, even 20 years later. There are many scars that I have, but a scar simply represents the place where Jesus' love has been. In the midst of building a relationship with the Lord, guess what He even gave me the courage to tell my dad that I was pregnant. The fact that this child had a heartbeat is what caused me to coward on the abortion and even suicide. It's amazing how God works. Her name is Diamond Alexis, and she's 25 years old today. My God, I can't imagine life without Diamond. I'm so thankful she had a heartbeat. It saved her life as well as mine. As I got a little older, I begin to realize how rich my parents life was. For many years it was defined by drugs, alcohol, and misery. But I realized that I had learned so much from both of them. Mama and daddy taught us what not to do. I realized how loved I was and I know in my heart that if they had the opportunity to have done things differently, they would have. But growing up in the way that I did, taught me how to be merciful to people.

It taught me how to appreciate what I have because I know what if feels like to not have anything at all. It taught me what honor looks like. Most importantly, it taught me how to lay my life down - as Jesus did for me. With the help of the Lord, I finally won the victory over my enemy - Satan! Yes, I have places that are still healing, but in Jesus, I am whole. I am free!

I want to encourage you that there is nothing too hard for God. You no longer have to hide. He sees and knows everything about you. Allow yourself to open your heart before the Lord because He's waiting. He wants to heal and restore and love on you in ways you could never imagine. He wants to redeem your life from sin. It doesn't matter if it was deliberate sin, or the sins of others that have control over your life. You can repeat this simple prayer: *Lord, forgive me of my sins and be my Lord and Savior. Show me who you are and reveal yourself to me in a way that I can understand. Help me to hate what you hate, and love what you love. In Jesus' name, Amen.*

Now it's time to FORGIVE YOURSELF. Ask God to help you to forgive yourself for choices you regret making or the unforgiveness you've held on to. Maybe you're holding on to the pain that has stolen your joy! Declare your freedom in the Name of Jesus! It takes one day at a time and sometimes one step at a time, but with God anything is possible. I'm a testament to that truth. God Bless!

"I don't always feel joyful, and sometimes it's hard to find a reason to be thankful, but when I recall how big our God is and what He's already done, it shifts my perspective and stirs up my faith."

A Victorious Faith Walk

TIFFANY TEMPLE

*T*he water was rising, but so was my faith. It was the morning of August 12, 2016—the second day of continuous heavy rain. It was also supposed to be the first day of my son's senior year of high school, but the school system canceled the start of school because of high water and dangerous road conditions. I was told to stay home from work and prepare for the worst. My dad, George, was out and about getting things prepared for him and mom, Sharalean, when he stopped by my house to chat with me over a cup of coffee as the rain continued to fall. We thought it would be a typical Louisiana rainy day with high water and power outages, but by mid-morning things were getting worse and the rain never stopped pouring from the sky. By mid-day, flooding had begun along the Comite and Amite rivers. My mother, my sister and her family had evacuated their homes to find refuge at mine. My dad stayed back as long as he could to place furniture and appliances as high as possible. Earlier, he parked his truck a couple of miles on higher ground away from their house so that once he decided to leave—when the waters entered the house—he waded through the water to his truck and came to my house. We all celebrated that he made it. We prayed together and hunkered down for the night. I was sitting on the sofa watching the news reports of what was being called the "One Thousand Year Flood". It was then I remembered a Christian magazine that was delivered unusually early featuring a pastor in South Carolina who witnessed angels protecting his home from the same type of floodwaters. As I read the featured article, I became more confident in believing the truth of God's word in Psalm 91. We were protected!

The next morning, I woke up to my sister yelling, "Wake up! Wake up! The water is here!" I woke up in disbelief because I knew I had experienced a breakthrough moment in prayer just a few hours ago. I opened the front door to see the water rushing down the street, vehicles stalled in the water, boats filled with people floating through, and trucks driving too fast sending waves of water into my front yard. This was the moment I had to remember the reason God blessed me with this house.

My sister, Candace, had been a successful Realtor for five years before I got serious about purchasing my first home. In 2010, I moved home with my parents to save money and repair my finances. In 2015, I was finally motivated to start the homebuying process by the fact that my son, Triston, would be graduating from high school in 2 years and likely moving far away. I wanted him to have a place of his own to return home for holidays and semester breaks. Two years would give us enough time to establish "home".

Candace and I began the homebuying process with a lender who helped me get my finances in order. I was stacking up cash and holding it in the bank as a sort of security blanket except there was no security in it. I was actually operating with a poverty mindset that I had to hold on to every drop of every penny. The lender was direct and helpful in her guidance. She gave me the kick in the butt I needed with her no-nonsense approach. It took no time for me to be in a position to purchase my first home. During the summer of 2015, Candace and I placed bids on 5 homes and lost every single bid. There was something special to me about each of those homes, and my hopes were high every single time only to endure the disappointment of losing the bid. I had been approved for $250,000.00, but I had a heart for working in the not-so-stable and not-so-lucrative non-profit sector, so I did not feel comfortable locking myself into that type of debt. I had to keep my bids low.

It became part of my daily routine to check the multiple listing service (MLS) for new real estate listings. One day, I saw a house on the site that looked like me. I had never had that feeling or thought before. It really looked like me. I had to see it! I called my sister and told her about it. She went to see the house on the site but told me it wasn't there. That was strange because I had just seen it on the website. I returned to the site to look again; just as she said, it was gone. I had saved a picture of the house, so my sister and I went to the house to see it for ourselves. It was close to the interstate and convenient to shopping and restaurants. The three-bedroom, two-bath house was small, but big enough with a yard small enough for me to manage and three crepe myrtle trees in the front yard. Crepe myrtles are my favorite! We went inside and everything was new and fresh. The house did not have the most modern updates, but everything was new. Candace and I had seen a lot of foreclosed homes that did not look as nice as this house. New indoor/outdoor paint, new appliances, new cabinets, new carpet, new flooring, new shelving and pegboards in the storage, new everything. My heart was bursting with confidence that this was my home. I sat on the floor of the living room and rested against the wall. My sister was checking out things around the house, as good Realtors do, and said, "Tiff, this feels different." I said, "I know. This feels like it's mine." We both smiled at each other and left with the agreement that we would place a winning bid. My sister took the little sister liberty of bidding $3,000 more than I wanted to bid, and we won! We were so excited and thankful to God. We told our mom but kept it a secret from my dad and son because I wanted to surprise them. It was August 21, 2015, two years before my son, Triston, graduated high school, and I was sitting there, closing on my first home with no co-signer. God did it! My proud sister was on one side of me and my friend's husband, Jeff, was the lender. We laughed and celebrated the entire time! I knew Jeff because he worked closely in support of his wife, my friend, Jennifer who is the founder of The Life of a Single Mom, so this was a victory for all of us. Jennifer would tell you that single mothers are half as likely as married couples to own a home, but I love to see women all over the world shattering those type of grim statistics by the grace of God every day.

Candace and I went out for lunch to celebrate then executed the plan to surprise our dad. It wasn't unusual for my father to meet my sister at some of the properties she showed for safety measures. We figured that's how we'd surprised him. She told him she needed him to come with her to view a house. He thought he was doing what he'd always done, showing up at one of her properties to ensure she was safe. Little did he know he was showing up to *my* new home. However, my presence was not common. Yet, he still didn't think anything of it. We asked him what he thought of the house, and he gave us so much positive feedback, which made me feel good about it. I held up the key and told him it was *mine*. He was so confused, but within a matter of seconds, the emotions began flowing. He told me he was proud of me. I was happy that he was proud of me, and to be honest, I was proud of myself.

Later that day, after football practice, we brought Triston to the house and surprised him. It was a glorious day! We didn't move in right away. I felt a strong conviction to bless the house before I moved any furniture in it. I knew God had given me this home to serve a purpose: a place of refuge, peace, and prayer. My prayer warrior mom helped me invite folks and plan a house blessing. We gathered in my empty house and prayed through every room. It was powerful. Months prior, my friends from Chicago (Ana and Liz), surprised me with a beautiful wooden plaque as a seed of faith for my new home. The handcrafted plaque read, "As iron sharpens iron, so a friend sharpens a friend. Proverbs 27:17." I had everyone in attendance sign the back of the plaque. It became my home's guestbook and provided a way for my friends to join us for the house blessing even though they were hundreds of miles away. Afterwards, we began moving my things in so that by Labor Day, Triston and I would be fully moved in. The first thing I hung on the wall was a picture my sister-friend, Sarah, gave me as a seed of faith as I was believing God for a home. The picture was a beautifully framed word art that read, "Bless this house with love and laughter." I remember Triston sprawled out on the same floor I sat on when I first entered the house. He looked around and said, "Mom, you really made this house a home." That moment was better than surprising him. It was an answered prayer!

A few weeks after moving in, I met my wonderful neighbors. All of them were much older, except Rachel who rented the house on my right. There was an older couple, Betty and Mac, who lived across the street from me. They quickly became my very own "Neighborhood Watch Captains". One day, while checking our mailboxes, Mr. Mac told me that the lady who lived there before me was the first and only homeowner. Her name was Leah, and she was a retired school teacher. Things apparently became tough for her when her adult daughter with special needs moved away to Georgia. As Mr. Mac continued, he seemed to understand from my facial expressions that this was all very new to me. Then he dropped a bombshell, "She committed suicide in that house." My face must have looked horrified because he stopped telling me the story. Our conversation ended abruptly and awkwardly as we both walked back to our homes. I was indeed shocked at the tragedy that had taken place, but at the same time I was excited at the leading of the Holy Spirit and my obedience to have my home blessed before any possession of mine entered the house.

Then there was Mr. Gordon. He lived diagonally across the street from me on the corner. He operated a windshield repair company from his garage where the proceeds benefited the homeless. Visiting his home was like entering a museum. He had been a very successful businessman. His walls were filled with pictures of him with every Louisiana Governor of his generation, celebrities and even a couple of U.S. Presidents. Talking with him was like opening an encyclopedia. It was always apparent that he and his wife lived a full life. When I met him, his wife was living in a nursing home so I never had the privilege of meeting her before her death. On one of his visits to my home, he told me it was refreshing that he finally had a neighbor with whom he could fellowship.

I met Rachel from next door and Robert from across the street when I invited my block of neighbors to my Christmas Open House. Rachel brought a gift that still has a special place in my living room, a pillow that says, "PEACE". Peace! Remember, my home is a place of refuge, peace and prayer! Rachel and Robert stayed and played games with my family and friends then joined us for candlelight caroling down the street. It was a wonderful night! I moved into the house in September of 2015 and although it had only been a short time since I'd been in the house, it was already living up to everything I knew it would be.

In the months to come, extraordinary things would take place at my home. One of which took place in January of 2016, I decided to obey God again by opening my home for small group Bible study. I could not shake the thought of something happening in our society that would prevent us from gathering in church buildings and how important it would be for believers to have a place to gather.

"And let us not neglect our meeting together, as some
people do, but encourage one another, especially now that
the day of his return is drawing near."
Hebrews 10:25 (NLT)

Remember my home is a place of PRAYER! Pray is certainly what we did! We made new friends and grew deeper connections with old friends. We did outreaches together, went on a cruise together, walked through difficult seasons together, celebrated each other, had church meet-ups, coffee hangouts and lived life together with Jesus at the center of it all. One of those new friends, became one of my dearest friends. Danielle lived in the adjacent neighborhood, and we would meet up before the chickens, at 4:45am, every weekday morning for a 45-minute walk. We solved all our problems, your problems and the world's problems in those 45 minutes. The truth is we were taking ground for Jesus with every step we took. As a matter of fact, I believe that's part of the reason God spared our homes during the flood. Both of our homes were places of REFUGE.

When I purchased my home, I knew that it was to be a place of refuge, peace and prayer. When the flood water of 2016 began to rise, and I saw it with my own eyes, I immediately beckoned Triston to join me in prayer. My parents, my sister and her family were packing up, and we were about to start placing things in the loft when I stopped and pulled Triston to the side. I explained to him that we were about to take authority over this storm by the power of Jesus. I told him that we are a family and God gave us this house to be a place of refuge, peace and prayer and that no matter what anybody else in this house thinks, we have the responsibility and power to declare what shall be. Triston and I stood in our home with waters rising outside and prayed to God for divine protection. Then we joined everyone in packing up to evacuate. Mr. Mac and Mrs. Betty stayed behind and kept in touch with me via text message. We drove through high water to the nearest McDonald's to get some breakfast and determine our next steps. It was heartbreaking to see everyone frantically doing the same. We went to a shelter, but it was nearly full and none of us wanted to stay there. While we hung out there for a while, my dad and Triston went to check on our properties. I'll never forget my daddy demonstrating with his fingers that the water was 3 inches from my door. With the rain continuing to fall and the floodwaters still moving across the city, we decided to head further northwest to Alexandria. We found a hotel. I connected with a friend, Sandy, who hosted us for dinner, let us wash clothes and relax for a few hours with her family. The phone reception was terrible so I could not reach Mr. Mac and Mrs. Betty until after we got word that the water had receded enough to get back to Baton Rouge. Mr. Mac and Mrs. Betty confirmed what we had contended for by faith, our home did not flood and neither did theirs or Robert's. Rachel had purchased a home and moved out before the flood, but the empty house took on water. The homes on all three sides of me took on water, but God spared my home. It was then that my home became a place of refuge for my family as they began the journey of rebuilding their flooded homes. For the next 5 months, all seven of us absorbed every nook and cranny of my house.

I had been working at The Life of a Single Mom since the start of 2016, so I was in a fortunate position to support many families, including my own, through this difficult time. My Bible study group continued to meet, and Danielle and I continued to walk our neighborhood each morning. One time, we walked in the evening just so I could get away from my new full house for a little while. On one of those walks, Danielle told me about a book she was reading with her book club and invited me to join as she was going to be hosting the book talk at her home this particular time. She added that she would invite two other ladies from our Bible study, Tawanda and Jennifer. This further deepened our connection leading to us becoming part of this book club of remarkable women living out God's plans for victorious living.

While I don't believe this home is my forever home, I know that it has a purpose and is a gift from God. I am thankful for every inch of it, every precious memory that fills it and every foot that has crossed its threshold. I am thankful for the times food and water have been plentiful and the times everything seemed dried up because it helped me see the miracle of God's provision. I'm thankful for having the responsibility of homeownership that humbled me to lean on the help of family and friends from time to time. I'm thankful for every tear shed, every gut-busting laughter, every prayer meeting, every game night, every spa party, every gathering and every overnight guest. I'm thankful for the lonely nights because it helped me appreciate the nights of a full house. I'm thankful for Triston coming home from university and taking my parking spot because this is his home. I'm thankful that the purchase of this home has marked my life with stories of victory that will make you shout, "Won't He do it!" because that means my victory points you to Jesus giving Him the glory for what He has done.

As I continue this victorious walk of faith, I look forward to the day I marry the man with whom I get to live out a purpose-filled journey of bringing joy, help, healing, and peace to our families and the world together. Our home will be an even bigger blessing with an even greater purpose. I'm convinced that my eyes have not seen neither have my ears heard all the great things God will do!

If you are reading this and connecting to the fact that I am a single mother, I especially want you to rejoice always, pray continually and give thanks in all circumstances. These three things have made all the difference in my journey! It's also essential to be in community with other believers who help you recall God's faithfulness and remind you to believe what your heart already knows. We need friends who not only help you see blind spots, but pry your eyes open when we are too stubborn to see. It is crucial that we create time and space to gather together and encourage one another, as Paul instructed us in Hebrews 10. The company you keep makes a difference in your faith walk.

I don't always feel joyful, and sometimes it's hard to find a reason to be thankful, but when I recall how big our God is and what He's already done, it shifts my perspective and stirs up my faith. I have victory in my faith walk, and I am forever grateful to God for His kindness towards me. When faced with challenging times, I remind myself that *as long as He's still feedin' 'dem birds, I know He's gon' take care of me!*

"My doctor told me not to live in the 'what if' of life. He advised me to just live. I made it up in my mind that I was going to live."

Healing Victory

BETTY LODGE

*I*n October 2012, I was diagnosed with cancer of the colon. I had lymphoma in my colon, and according to my provider, lymphoma isn't supposed to be in your colon. My doctor also told me that having lymphoma in your colon is a rarity; they see this in about 1% of patients.

Before I was diagnosed, I was going about my life as I normally did. I began not feeling like myself in the summer of 2012. By September 2012, I began to feel pain in my lower abdomen. Over the course of several months, I went to see one doctor after another. That's when the process of elimination began. Most of them performed numerous tests on me, trying to rule out all they could. After a series of tests, I decided to see my Gynecologist, who couldn't diagnose me and advised me to see a Gastroenterologist. So, I did. When I went there, I explained everything I'd gone through, what I was experiencing physically, and the results that landed me at a Gastro-Intestinal (GI) appointment. They performed a CT scan, and saw something on the scan. Therefore, they wanted to take it a step further by scheduling me for a colonoscopy.

During the waiting period, I prayed earnestly. I felt something was really wrong and they weren't getting to the bottom of it. The pain I felt in my stomach was worsening to the point of being unable to sit comfortably. I had to lean on one side of my body or the other to sit down; otherwise, lying down was my only other option. Something told me this was going to be a journey. I remember talking to the Lord one day, telling Him, *I want you to lead and I'm going to follow. I trust you and I need to know what's wrong with me because something is wrong.* **I was afraid.** I didn't want anyone to know what I was feeling, not even my husband.

In that month of waiting, the pain transitioned into a hotspot. When I touched the right side of my stomach, it was hot to the touch. It was strange and hard to explain. I tried to explain it to my GI doctor. One day during church service, I was standing and singing along during worship when I heard a voice. It was just one word: *fire.* I heard it so clearly that I asked, *Lord, is this you?* The next thing that came to me was, **my fire.** I kept saying to myself, *Lord, I receive your healing.* I began to cry, then whispered to my husband, "The Lord said this hot spot is **His fire.**" He said, "What?" I told him, "I believe the Lord is healing me."

After my colonoscopy, my GI doctor told myself and my husband that he'd seen many colons but never one that looked like this. He panicked and wanted to schedule me with the surgeon for the next morning. As he walked from behind the curtain, and made a phone call, I laid there thinking, *oh my God, what is going on?* My appointment was set for 8 a.m. the next day. **That's when the journey began.**   At that moment, I understood why my GI doctor was so alarmed at how my colon looked. God was healing my body and *His fire* had burned the cancer which made my colon look abnormal. Instantly, *I told the Lord that I Trust him and that I would follow him on the journey.* **Fear left me.**

After my appointment with the colon surgeon, she said, "From what the GI doctor and I see, we are thinking this is lymphoma, which is not something we see in the colon. I don't want to put fear in you, but I'm pretty sure this is cancer."

First, I was told it was fast growing, then I was told it wasn't fast growing. At any rate, it had to be treated and removed as soon as possible. I was supposed to have surgery in November 2012, but my appointment was canceled. After consulting with an Oncologist, the surgeon told me they couldn't perform the surgery. They referred me to another oncologist and I had to undergo a series of tests again. The oncologists wanted me to go through chemotherapy first. In all of that, I *knew* I was *healed*. I returned to my surgeon and begged her to allow me to have the surgery. I didn't need chemo and radiation, then have the surgery. I just wanted the surgery. The Holy Spirit told me that this was a foreign object that needed to be removed. The surgeon advised me that she and a group of other doctors would meet to discuss my case and decide from there.

I knew I was diagnosed with cancer, but I *refused* to claim it! Whatever was there, I knew God had burned it out, and that's why He reminded me of **HIS fire**. On the other hand, my husband was so broken because of the diagnosis. Accompanying me on my doctors' visit was difficult for him. I could hardly talk with the doctors about my condition because Freddie would get so emotional. But I was **walking in my healing**. I knew I had the victory over cancer, and I would continue to stand on God's Word. I would go through everything the doctors wanted, but I knew I was healed. No one was going to make me claim it. Many negative reports came my way from the moment I was diagnosed, but I was on a journey with God.

I kept my eyes on the Lord, above all circumstances and didn't allow myself to get in the mix of things going on around me with the doctors and reports. My family might've thought I was crazy or in denial because I told them to stop telling people I had cancer. I *knew* what I was going through, but I also *knew* God was taking care of it and I would be fine. Cancer was something I *refused* to say I had.

When the surgeon called me back, she had good news! She said, "Betty, your case was put before a panel of 30 doctors. I told them what you, as the patient, wanted, and it was decided that I could do the surgery first." I was so thankful because now I didn't have to do chemo and radiation first. At this point, I knew all I needed was the *foreign object* removed from my body as the Lord had spoken to me. I told my husband the good news. He asked me what would happen afterward. "Are you going to deny chemo?" I told him, "I don't need any of that because *I'm **healed**.*" He thought I was crazy too!

After the surgery in December 2012, I went back for my follow-up in January 2013. My oncologist said, "My partners and I don't know what to do with you. I'm going to be honest; this is rare. If you could, would you be willing to go to MD Anderson? We want them to review your case and tell us what to do." I told them I was willing to go to MD Anderson in Houston. All of my test results and samples from my colon were sent to the medical staff at MD Anderson. The samples were scheduled to be retested and a comparison analysis was ordered.

I was living in Baton Rouge, LA. For my first visit to MD Anderson in Houston, I was supposed to stay there for four days to complete all the requested testing. I was informed that the cancer was only in stage one and nowhere else in my body. After all the testing was done, I went in to see the doctor and he said, "Mrs. Lodge, Mr. Lodge, we are so happy that you came to us. We've done everything we needed to do and we see **No signs of cancer in your body**." *"You would've been having chemo and radiation for no reason."* I praised God right there! The Lord told me I was healed **before** the doctors even announced it to me. There was nothing else for him to treat.

My oncologist wanted me to continue being his patient so that he could monitor me for the next five years. In my first year as his patient, I saw him twice. They continued testing me and sent me to a Radiologist to determine if I needed to do radiation. I was told I didn't need to do radiation, that I was *cancer free!* In my second year, I went twice again. In my third year as his patient, he told me I only needed to see him once. Between those times, I prayed and never let anyone tell me I had cancer. Anytime fear would try to rise up in me, I'm reminded of **His** *fire* and that **I Trust Him**. My doctor told me not to live in the 'what if' of life. He advised me to live. At that point, I made up my mind that I was going to live. Not just live, but live a victorious life which includes servicing others. Psalm 91 taught me how to trust God and have faith. My daily confession was I *Trust you* Lord and I'm under your covering.

In 2017, I stopped seeing my oncologist at MD Anderson in Houston. He said, "Honestly, I didn't know if I would see something come up or not in these five years. But you have amazed all of us." I told him God healed me, and I was so thankful for him and his team. As he released me in November 2017, he told me, "We're here if you need us. But I don't think you will." He told me to go live my life, and I am.

God healed me, but this isn't the only thing He healed me from. He also healed me from breast cancer prior to the lymphoma in my colon. Breast cancer has run in my family. I've had several biopsies on my breasts, and for a while, everything was benign.

Around 2004, I saw my breast specialist, who performed a mammogram after I told her I'd been having breast pain. After the testing, they told me they saw cancer cells. They sent the sample off for further testing, and she advised me to come in for a removal. From there, I was set up for surgery. I was in total fear. I remember walking into my kitchen, sitting at the island, and crying. My husband hadn't made it home yet. I didn't know what I was going to do.

As I sat there, I asked God, *Lord, what am I going to do?* This was the one thing I was hoping and praying passed me. I walked to my front door, pulled the curtain back, and looked out. I heard a voice say, *if you have cancer, what are you going to do?* I said, *I'm going to trust you and tell others of your goodness, Lord.* **All fear left me at that very moment and there was a peace that came over me.**

At that time, I led a bible study group, and I shared my diagnosis with them. We prayed together, believed in a miracle, and waited on the Lord to move. One of the ladies from the group took me to my appointment. As we waited in the lobby, I noticed another lady who was alone and waiting to have her surgery. I started a conversation with her and began encouraging her to have faith and she would be okay. The lady accompanying me told everyone in our small group that she was amazed at how I encouraged someone else right before I had to go into surgery. What she didn't understand was that I had **peace** from God, which shifted my focus from myself and allowed me to see the need of someone else!

I had the procedure done, and the removed substance was sent to the lab for testing. I went back to my breast specialist, and she apologized for recommending the procedure because the testing came back negative. **I didn't have breast cancer!** She said she and her partner looked at the original scan and saw something worth the procedure. She went on to say she couldn't explain it, but she was indeed sorry. I told her that God had to show me something. *This incident was just for me.* This was the first of my journey with needing to **trust** God with my health.

Because of the incident with breast cancer, I wasn't so fearful of the lymphoma in the colon. God had already shown me that He would take care of me. I was on a *journey of trust.* He allowed these things to happen so I would learn how to trust Him. The only way to get through this was to stay focused on Him. Even when doubt arose, I had to remind myself that God was in control.

Going through the process wasn't always easy, but my faith helped me through it. Now, I was going to tell everyone of His goodness!

I've gone through many things in my life that required me to have faith. My husband and I dated for two years before we married in 1983. I was 25 years young. We had some rough years and that's where I feel like my faith journey began.

We both came from a religious background, but neither of us had a relationship with the Lord. While we were dating, sometime in 1981, my husband found his faith in the Lord, and I became curious. I remember going to church with him one day, and it felt weird. However, I saw a great change in his life. One day, I went home for lunch, but before I went back to work, I had this sudden urge, which I'd never had, to kneel down. I kneeled down at my sofa by the door and said, *Lord, if this is real, show me who you are.* I got up and continued with my day. Music is something I've always loved. I got into my car and headed back to work. As usual, I put on some music, but something told me to turn it off.

My life began to change after that prayer. I gave my life to the Lord, and He revealed that Freddie was the man I should marry and Freddie knew it too but was running from it. A year later, Freddie and I got married. I was so angry with him the day he proposed to me. I had gone to the church that he, too, was attending, and I saw some girl there with him. It looked like they were more than friends. *Are they dating?* I thought to myself. That evening at home, I prayed that the Lord would remove every feeling I had for him in my heart. I needed to go in another direction. I wanted to be free of him, although the Lord had already told me he was my husband. That evening, he came over. I opened the door to let him in and sat on the sofa. He kneeled down in front of me and proposed to me. I looked at him like he was crazy. I told him what I had just prayed and he told me what the Lord had spoken to him about marrying me. He said the Lord said," if you don't do it today, you will lose her".

When you are young, you're naive. I should've seen the signs, but I was young. We got married, and I realized that he grew up with a completely different lifestyle from me. I came from a two-parent household, and family was a big deal. My husband's parents were divorced at a very young age so, he didn't have the same family roots as I had with a two-parent home. He said he didn't understand why my family was so close and it made him feel uneasy.

We separated a few years after we got married. He needed to determine if he wanted to be married or be single. At the time, we had two young children together. We stayed separated for one year and nine months. **It was rough.** He was hands-on financially. He made sure everything was taken care of, but he wasn't present, and I didn't want him present because he had a choice to make. I wasn't going to live assuming or wondering whether or not he was being faithful to me. I also didn't want the children to grow up in a home full of arguing. It was a hurtful time, but necessary.

I'd gone to the courthouse to get some information on filing for a divorce. My eldest sister had a conversation with me. She said it didn't make sense to file for divorce and asked me why I was. She wondered if a divorce was going to give me some kind of relief. She talked me through it and suggested I give it more time. He was asking to come back home, but I wasn't ready to let him come home. I knew I needed to pray about it and make a decision myself.

During that time, our son fell ill. We didn't know what was happening with him, but he almost died. He was six years old. His body was full of disease. He had chickenpox, scarlet fever, strep throat, and other illnesses he was experiencing simultaneously. His head and face were swollen. Many doctors were seeing him, trying to figure out how to treat him. None of the antibiotics were working. He had been in the hospital for weeks. He couldn't talk or swallow. We were so afraid. Due to the disease, they only allowed two people in the room with him. We had to be dressed in specific clothing to go in and see him, and when we came out, we had to strip out of the clothing.

A friend of mine had a friend who lived in California. She wanted to call her so we all could pray together. The doctors told us that they didn't know what else they could do if the medication didn't work. My prayer group and my friend's friend prayed with us. We began to pray before she stopped and asked, "I don't mean to get in your business, but are you and your husband together?"

"No," I said.

"Humph. I don't want to hurt you, but I feel I need to tell you something."

She began talking and saying things that were impossible for her to know because I hadn't shared any of these things with anyone. Not even our mutual friend.

She went on to tell me that my son was supposed to die. But he shall live and not die. She asked me to repeat that with her, and I did. I was crying as she was praying. When she was done praying, she said she wanted to meet me and my husband if she ever came to Louisiana. She told me that the Lord had him and I together for a reason. I agreed to meet with her if she was ever in town.

The next day, my son woke up and could talk and eat. We were amazed, as were the doctors. His pediatrician said, "I don't know what happened overnight, but the prayer and antibiotics worked. I didn't think he was going to pull through." My son was in the hospital for a total of a month. When he came home, he had all kinds of tubes and IVs. He still had to be isolated.

After this, my husband and I reunited as a family. I had to learn how to trust my husband again, which was hard. Six or seven months later, the lady who prayed over my son with us came into town and conversed with my husband and me. She said that our marriage was meant to be. She began speaking to my husband, taking him back to his childhood. She asked him about his childhood and was on point with everything she said. She told us that our lives would be a testimony for other people. She asked me if she could have a conversation with him in private and that there were some things she needed to discuss with him alone. So, I left the room. I don't know what she said to my husband, but my marriage began healing from that day.

We've now been married for 40 years. Going through life with him, he said he wasn't accustomed to seeing family that showed each other the kind of love as my family showed. By praying and allowing God to change his life, he has learned how to live a different life.

The enemy was trying to destroy the family God created, but I fought for my marriage and family. It wasn't easy allowing him back into my life. When I couldn't trust my husband, and there were many times that I felt as though I couldn't, I told God that I would trust him and needed God to change my husband into the man he needed to be for me and my children. By praying and allowing God to change Freddie's life, he has learned how to live a different life and become a spiritual husband and father. He shared with me that he asked God to teach him how to be the husband and father he needed to be for his family. I've seen this change in him and there is nothing that he wouldn't do for his family. Before the change, he was always a good provider, but self-centered. Being a good provider is great, however, the children and I wanted more of him; not just what he could give us. God taught him how to give of himself to his family, enjoy the time he spends with us and love us unconditionally. I'm so thankful for the husband that God has given me. *God changed him!*

Strengthening your faith isn't an easy thing. But whatever you're going through, you must drop it at the cross. You have to give it over to the Lord. Don't pick it back up. Listen to God, and spend time with Him so that you can develop trust in Him. God wants us to be obedient and trust Him.

You have to get to a place close to Him. God gave me an analogy once. I was walking in a park, and he showed me a shadow and told me, "When you're under the protection of the shadow, that's Me. But when you remove yourself from that shadow, you're outside of me." You have to let God fix it. The shadow of God is where you should stay.

No matter what I've gone through, everything comes back to trusting the Lord. We don't know what life is going to bring us, but there's always purpose in it, and trusting the Lord is mandatory. God took me from one level of trust to the next. When I look back, I see just how God showed me that He could be trusted. God not only healed my body, but he healed my family. No matter what happens in life, I will **ALWAYS** have the victory *In Christ*!

"We no longer have to wallow in self-pity. Each day, we have the opportunity to discover more and more of our worth. I've decided to be more optimistic than pessimistic and walk in victory."

Victory Over Family Matters

VALARIE DOWNING

Every family goes through challenges that are off putting to some but quite normal for others. I witnessed family dysfunction in every level of my life. In 1965, I was born into a home where my father physically and mentally abused my mother, for many years. My father was a foreman at a chemical plant in the 50s and 60s. He was a drinker, gambler and a womanizer. He fathered children outside of their marriage and put my mom through living hell. My father would work all week, gamble, drink and have his women on evenings and weekends. Over time, the routine became a part of life and my mom just endured it. These were the first few years of my life. As an adult there are a few memories I recall from that young age. I remember sitting on my father's lap and he let me taste the brown liquor in his glass. I vaguely recall my mom saying not to do that. Then there was the Easter we were visited by some Nuns from the Catholic Church who gave us many things, including a big chocolate egg wrapped in colorful foil with plastic grass and smaller chocolate candy nestled in. It was so pretty. Little did I know, my mom was crying out for help to feed and clothe us, while my father lived in the same household. There was a Sunday my mom and I went out and when we got back, he would not open the door. We were locked outside, and he would not let my brother or sister let us in.

One day, my mom told us, "I need y'all to get ready to get in the car." It was early afternoon. She went into the house, brought out a bunch of clothes, and placed them on the backseat. I remember sitting in the backseat on top of the clothes. *She was leaving my father.* She no longer wanted to be a battered woman. She wanted freedom!

On our drive to our place of refuge, my grandmother's house, our father somehow was able to chase us down in his car and tried to run us off the road. My mother never wavered, she had to have been scared out of her wits, but she just drove faster. I knew, even at that young age, he could have killed us. She made it to my grandmother's driveway and started blowing her horn, my grandmother came out with a shotgun! She was ready to shoot, asking no questions! Thank God for safety. Thank God my mother left when she did. The Lord protects us from harm.

Proverbs 18:10 (NKJV) The name of the Lord is a strong tower; the righteous run to it and are safe.

Growing up, my mom never bashed my father in our faces. In the divorce decree, my mom was supposed to receive $25.00 monthly in child support from my father. He never paid her anything, yet she continued to raise the three of us. As time went on, I entered kindergarten and lived among my siblings and cousins on my mom's side of the family. I have many happy memories of playing outside shooting marbles, racing barefoot and learning how to play spades!!! (Lol) Yes, we were taught young! (Lol) Living in a mobile home just steps away from my grandmother's front door, was the best thing that could have happened in our situation. She taught me without words, how to take care of others, I even learned how to make cottage cheese.

There was dysfunction there, too. I had an uncle and one of his older sons, whom my grandmother loved dearly and would spend lots of money to buy liquor and cook food for his visits from New Orleans. We spent days cleaning every corner of the house, for our 'special guest.' Sadly, my uncle battled alcoholism in his life too and they disappointed her many times by not showing up. However, the occasions they did show up were fun-filled and exciting. My uncle and cousin were great storytellers. What a time we had!

There is no place like home.

In 1976, my mom bought our home. Imagine, a single black woman working as a cook, saving and purchasing on her own a home during those years. She found a house in an adjacent neighborhood to the one her older sister lived in. The house she found had to be renovated even though it was fairly new. The previous occupants destroyed the home. The house had been the scene of domestic violence.

> Matthew 12:43-45 (KJV When an unclean spirit comes out of a man, and passes through arid places seeking rest and does not find it. Then says, 'I will return to the house I left.' On its return, it finds the house vacant, swept clean and put in order. Then it goes and brings with it seven other spirits more wicked than itself, and they go in and dwell there;

As we prepared to move in, my mom was so excited and exhausted. I remember spending all day at Butler Furniture Company while she picked out furniture for the entire house. As I look back on this as an adult, it still blows my mind to realize my mother was amazing. She was determined to live her best life and raise our family despite all odds.

During my next few years, I began to see fewer days of play and more days of responsibility. My sister went off to college and my brother lived with us on and off during those years. Since it was mainly me and my mom, my life as a latchkey kid began when I was in the 5th grade.

My mom raised me to be very independent. Since my mom left early in the morning for work each day, I had to get myself up, get dressed and make sure to not miss the bus or have a situation where she had to come up to my school. That just wasn't acceptable. Sometimes, she worked two or three jobs to ensure we had what we needed. I spent a lot of time alone, becoming my own best friend. This is when I started to see my brother fight with drug addiction and how my mother was living angry, scared for him, and sad. Thankfully the Lord kept his hand on my brother and he eventually overcame drug addiction and lived a long life in Christ until he passed away a few years ago. I was blessed to have had my sister during those years. She had since married and had a family of her own, but she spent a lot of her life caring for me. As I got older, I realized she also had battle scars from childhood that no one ever addressed. Through the grace of God, she became and is an awesome woman. I love my sister so much.

I started high school in 1979, this was when high went from 9th -12th grade. During that summer I got a job at IHOP on State St, by LSU in Baton Rouge, Louisiana and started a 4-year journey of working weekends and summers. My sister and my brother in-law spent countless hours and lots of gas giving me rides to and from work. They endured hardship I'm sure, for the sacrifices they made for me.

My mom is a very private person which made my high school years very different from my classmates. I had always had to stay indoors. If any of my classmates/friends came to our house, we went to the end of the driveway. I couldn't invite them inside. When my mother was not home, I could not answer the door and couldn't give out our telephone number to anyone, either.

As senior year was coming close, there was an incident that I had lied to my teacher about. My mom and I went to her house. When we got to the door, I was already sick to my stomach. I had lied, got caught in the lie and now had to account for it. What happened next shook me. The teacher called me a very bad name, belittled me, and told me I was nothing, etc. I don't recall my mom disagreeing or saying anything that would have even remotely told the teacher not to speak that way about me. She may have felt the same way.

I can now understand how she may have been embarrassed, ashamed, mad and disappointed in me.

I had sinned. Even though I knew little of the word of God, I knew lying was a sin. As I stood there, wanting to cry, weak, and humiliated, I uttered, I was sorry. There was nothing else in the conversation that involved my input, just my sorrow. I felt wounded beyond repair. The words that are spoken over us, whether good or bad, can be a blessing or they can be a curse. I harbored that pain for many years.

The sin of unforgiveness

It wasn't until I was 36 years old that I realized I had so much unforgiveness in my heart from that encounter with my teacher. I felt like no one cared about me, my future, or really anything about me for many years. I had lived being belittled, distressed, ashamed and reminded often of what my teacher had said about me. As my mom was going through her own battles, she too suffered behind closed doors but was able to overcome it. As I look at my mom today, I'm in awe of her. God was with us then and with us now.

One Sunday at church, my pastor said to the congregation, "If there is anyone who has hurt or offended you, I want you to come down, and we'll have someone come and stand in proxy. Tell them everything about what they've done that's hurt you so bad so that you can move on." I walked down to the altar. I was met by a woman who prayed with me. She told me that I was God's masterpiece and that He created me for good works in Christ Jesus, according to Ephesians 2:10 KJV. That scripture has stayed with me and became the benchmark for how I began to see life.

> *"We no longer have to wallow in self-pity. Each day, we have the opportunity to discover more and more of our worth. I've decided to be more optimistic than pessimistic and walk in victory."*

Marriage

I married a wonderful man. However, for years, I silently and unknowingly fought for affirmation from my husband. All I wanted was for him to tell me I was doing a good job, acknowledge my abilities and recognize me as his helpmate. My father never validated me because my parents divorced when I was young, and I had no relationship with him as I was growing up. Although my husband was doing everything in his power to show me love by taking care of me and protecting and providing for our children, that wasn't enough for me. Sometimes we can't see the forest for the trees. My husband and I struggled for years because I felt devalued as a wife and felt my voice was unheard. The dysfunction was now in my household. During these years, in our family, we wrestled with many of the same issues that were in my childhood. Gambling, drug addiction, poor health, mental illness and so much more.

I was blessed to connect with Monica through Bethany Church. She is also one of the co-authors of this book. We prayed about my not being affirmed by my father and my unknowingly trying to get affirmation from my husband. We prayed for years about all of our family matters. It has taken a lot of time to get to where I am today in Christ. Ultimately, it wasn't about my husband affirming or validating me. I had come to the understanding that the Lord established me. My responsibility was to gain a different perspective of who God uniquely created me to be.

Psalm 16:11 (NLT) 'You will show me the path of life; In Your presence is fullness of joy; At your right hand are pleasures forevermore.'

Identity

In my adult life, I know what God says about me. Even so, I still struggle with self-worth. This stems from the shame and embarrassment I carried for so many years. My remedy now for the constant struggle is to remain rooted in the word of God and surround myself with people who remind me of what God says about me. The low to no self-worth makes for a very active playground for Satan. The feeling that I'm not good enough, smart enough or what I have to say is not important enough to those around me, is something I struggle with even now. Gratefully, I'm not a person who wallows in self-pity. I've learned to shift my perspective to the way God see me and the truth of His Word concerning me. This has made it possible for me to be confident in how I carry myself.

Most people are envious of the things someone else has. That wasn't my issue. I felt unworthy, like my things are not good enough, and others won't see a value in them. This has led to a crippling behavior. I fear inviting people to my home. This really started about 10 years ago. I've never lived in a shabby place, but those complexes formulated all the way from childhood can rise at any point of our lives. I've fought this spirit of embarrassment and unworthiness for many years, but my victory comes when I turn my heart towards the goodness of God. When the focus of my heart changes, I become increasingly grateful that my God is enough. I am enough. I am His, and I am worthy of all the ways He has blessed me.

Luke 12:15(NLT) And He said to them, "Take heed and beware of covetousness, for one's life does not consist in the abundance of the things he possesses."

In my walk with God, I have been able to see my family's life being subject to multiple generational curses. There's alcoholism, gambling, sexual promiscuity, drugs, mental illness to name a few.

My mother has battled the same things I'm fighting, and because we've never talked about it, I never knew *how* to talk about it, let alone overcome it.

> Ephesians 6:12-13(NLT) 'For we do not wrestle against flesh and
> blood, but against principalities, against powers, against rulers of
> the darkness of this age, against spiritual host of wickedness in the
> heavenly places. Therefore take up the whole armor of God, that you
> may be able to withstand in the evil day, having done all to stand.'

I experienced unexpected childhood trauma because hurt people hurt other people. God has brought me through *my* lies, disobedience, sin, and things only He and I know about. I refuse to condemn my parents or anyone else any longer because I know how far God has brought me. I am not so holy and have lived so upright that I can remain angry or afford myself the space to be bitter about what someone has done to me. We've all been the villain in someone's story. We may think that what we've done to someone isn't that bad, but in someone else's eyes, they may be terribly wounded by us. We don't get to determine how bad we've hurt someone.

Life's Lessons

No matter how bad the pain is, we cannot remain resentful, and until we do our own self-reflection, moving on isn't an option. I'm appreciative of my mother regardless of the past. For years, my mother lived in condemnation. She was going through a very difficult time when I was younger. I remind her that God has renewed our relationship and the past is just that. I see her as victorious. I don't know if I could've endured her pain. My mother is successful, wonderful and to top it off, fabulous! I'm very proud of her. She raised us and gave life's lessons on work ethic, family dedication and love. I love how she dotes on me and my sister and accepts us as adult women, trusting us to help with her life/needs. When our brother was still with us, she was the same with him. I know that my mother would do *anything* for us, and I do my best to honor her. God has given me an abundance of forgiveness in my heart for her. I sought forgiveness from her, for the things I did that hurt her. The Lord has also allowed me to see the blessings of having my husband. I thank the Lord for the covering he provides, the love he gives me and expectant hope of many years to come. Thanking God for our 37 years of marriage.

God has allowed me to see the blessings in the trauma and not focus on the pain of the past.

No matter how bad things were, God has allowed me to see how good things are, resulting in my refusal to be bitter.

Victory

One of my greatest victories in life is how God healed my family. To see the Lord answer my prayer request to increase harmony in my family is incredible and moves me to tears. Now, we can be in the same room with no animosity. We can share the same space and experience peace, understanding, respect, and, most of all, genuine love. God can give you victory over your family matters, just like He did for me.

The moral of my story is that no matter what's hidden or the level of life you're living, there's always victory waiting to spring forth from inside you. We have the victory, through Jesus Christ!

My Shades of Victory Family

I've attended the same church with most of the ladies and small groups. These women have enriched my life in many ways. Betty and Monica taught me that God can do anything and the seasons we go through prepare us for the coming harvest. Good or bad, we live in transparency. They have helped me to become a better woman.

Through these women, God has allowed me to know, that I am strong, and no matter how weak I am, God can pick me up, and no matter the situation, He can turn it around!

You were born to be victorious, in the end, we win!

"For some, I realize being around too many people can be overwhelming; however, seeking out relationships with people has been paramount to my success in navigating this life. Jesus did not live life alone, nor should we."

Victory in Community

JENNIFER TAYLOR

*T*his was the product of what I prayed for. It was the first time I heard the clearest whispering voice telling me this was His intention for me. With the scariest faith and calmest of peace, I knew it was going to require me to be uncomfortable and do something that I had never done before. The thought of leaving the dark place that I grew to know, made me nervous. I was curious about what it would feel like to no longer experience this loneliness. The feelings of isolation were unpleasant, but the overwhelming peace He gave me positioned me toward hope. He pointed me back to Him. And He guided me towards community. Through this journey, I learned that He purposed me to not only be *in* community but to *be* the community for those around me. This is the detour that led me to find victory through community.

In January 2010, I took one of the biggest leaps of faith by quitting my job and started nursing school full-time. My husband, Marvin, and I prayed consistently the year before to ensure we heard this strong nudge correctly. If you have never questioned God before, congratulations to you. We had reasonable cause to question Him. We had been married for three years, had an incredible amount of debt and I still had collection agencies calling me several times a week. Not to mention, we were still living paycheck to paycheck. So, to say that we were comfortable going from two incomes to one would be a stretch. However, as God has always done in our lives, He made provisions for us.

My first encounter with finding my community was in nursing school. I was excited to be in the program and optimistic since nursing was my *calling*. I expected it to be easy for me since this was God's plan. I was completely wrong in this mindset and learned quickly that this was no cakewalk. I spent what felt like more hours studying than I did sleeping and yet still struggled to get Cs on my exams. Since I was considered a non-traditional nursing student at the ripe old age of twenty-nine and had already earned a bachelor's degree, I had an awareness of how I best comprehended information. In undergrad, I recorded the lectures and listened to them repeatedly. It was during nursing school that I quickly realized how important knowing how I learned was going to be for my success, so I went back to study habits that worked for me in the past. Listen. Write. Repeat. However, as consistent as I did this, it was not working. I read out loud, made charts, drawings, and rewrote what it felt like the entire textbook, but nothing changed. I was incredibly discouraged because I felt like a failure at something I had been called to do.

What I did not know until midterm was that I was not the only student not doing as well in this program. One day I overheard some of my classmates discussing their grades. After being invited into the conversation by someone asking me how I was doing on the tests, the attention quickly shifted towards me and my study habits for study advice, however, I did not feel like I was in any position to provide. I talked through the things that I did and the time that I spent doing them. Before I knew it, a study group was formed with a few of my classmates. The more we met and reviewed the information together, the more synergy we gained from one another. What I grew to understand about myself in the context of this study group was that I not only learned best in this environment, but we *all* thrived as evidenced by our test scores. This was the community that I needed and whether my classmates knew it or not, it was the community they needed as well.

After a few months, our study group began to evolve. The study group provided a safe space for transparent conversations as we realized that we were going through this experience together. We related to one another because we shared some of the same challenges whether that be financial, social, emotional, or spiritual. In the coming semesters, we welcomed new classmates into the group, enlarging our community. The successes of those in our study group were noticed by those not connected to us and the benefit of being a part of our community was notable. For this reason, we allowed anyone that wanted to be in our community to be a part. During various semesters, joining our study group was a last ditch effort for a few students to get the support they needed to make a passing grade to remain in the program. Unfortunately, because they were hesitant to join our community, they were not as successful as they could have been. This is the importance of being in a community. If you still have breath in your body, it is never too late for community. The time we spent studying together and the community we formed was the reason so many of us were victorious throughout the program and are certified, practicing nurses today.

By the time I was close to finishing the nursing program, most of my friends had gotten married and started families. It was difficult for me to stay connected to some of my friends during nursing school; however, there were a few of my old faithfuls who understood the commitment of time nursing school required of me. Occasionally when we had a break from school, I would connect with Red, who was my friend and college roommate. I learned that her son, Jeremiah, had been diagnosed with autism spectrum disorder. Though I do not think any of us had a clear understanding of what autism was, Marvin and I supported Red and Jeremiah by participating in the annual Autism Awareness walk. Throughout the years and the busyness of life, it seemed the Autism Walk was one thing we were able to do, and it allowed us to reconnect as if no time had passed. I grew to understand the challenges that this diagnosis presented for Red, as a parent. It seemed to devastate her, but she sought out a community, got a better understanding of the disease, and ensured her son had the resources necessary to be successful in the season he was in. Over time, I began to understand more as I had the opportunity to have more conversations with her and got to interact with Jeremiah. From ABA, accommodations, speech therapy, ADHD, IEP, and everything in between, there were terms that I was forced to learn to understand what Red was talking about when it concerned the challenges that she faced. I was privileged to observe her and walk with her through her son's diagnosis. Little did I know, being present for Red during that season would prepare me for an unexpected diagnosis of autism in my son, Elijah, a few years later. It was during this time that I realized my friendship with Red was the catalyst for the community she and I would build for one another as parents of children with autism.

It was the first Christmas Elijah could enjoy and remember, so I went all out to make sure everything was my vision of perfection. There were mountains of gifts wrapped in coordinated wrapping paper. I had anticipated this for weeks, so I am sure I was the most excited and working Marvin's last nerve. I was ready to take pictures and videos because I wanted to capture every moment so we could share it with our family and friends. Elijah seemed entertained with tearing the paper from the boxes, then anxiously waiting for the box to be opened so he could play with the toy. This would last about five to six minutes, then we took the toy in exchange for a wrapped gift for him to open. As a terrible two, it was not uncommon for him to have tantrums, so these tantrums were not cause for concern. So, when he had a tantrum with the toy being taken away from him, it was not surprising. We would give him another wrapped gift, the tantrum would dissipate, and with tears in his eyes, he would smile as he began to unwrap the next gift. We opened the box, allowed him to play with its contents, and moved on to the next present. The tantrum ensued. With each present, the tantrums and tears grew louder and more tumultuous than the last. Elijah grew more and more inconsolable with each present. This was something that I did not expect and became frustrated as I pondered what could be causing this. Marvin did not seem concerned, but with the episodes following each gift, after several boxes, we decided to stop and just allow him to play with the toys that were unwrapped. Elijah was content with that plan, but it was devastating to me. The behavior that I witnessed was something that I recalled being that of children with some type of disability. I was not certain, but with my previous experiences of working in a daycare and my mom having an in-home daycare for several years, I knew something was different.

Red, green, yellow, blue, black. Red, green, yellow, blue, black. Elijah would put all his cars in a straight line and in that order: red, green, yellow, blue, then black. When I played with him, I knew not to move the red car because it would cause a meltdown. Red was his favorite color. It was so much so that as he got older the other kids at daycare and his teachers knew that whatever it was whether it was scissors, crayons, or legos, Elijah must have the red one. It was not a preference, it was imperative. Many incidents occurred with him and either a student or a teacher that stemmed from Elijah not having the "red one".

As Elijah started school, I had so much anxiety surrounding how he was going to respond to the constant change in schedules, what I later learned were termed "transitions" that he did not do well with. It was not only at school though. Marvin was traveling a lot for work and with him being the more structured parent, this was always a tough time for Elijah. With me being the more "fly by the seat of my pants" type of parent, Elijah would have the same meltdowns at home that he would have at school when it was just the two of us. I learned from his teacher that she used a picture schedule at school so Elijah would know the structure of the day. She also provided him with a time frame for when things were due to change and would set that corresponding time on a timer, so he would know when it was time to transition. We adopted these practices at home to support Elijah with the transitions, so it provided a more structured environment for him and decreased our frustrations as well.

The early years were challenging. It felt like I was getting a call from the school every day because they could not de-escalate him and I needed to pick him up, to notify me that he caused bodily harm to someone, or that he was being suspended and would not be permitted to return for 3 days. As a first-time mom, I took this personal. I felt like a failure. Most days, the only thing I knew to do was pray. When Elijah was suspended for the second time, I reached out to Red. The conversation with her was exactly what I needed. She was so helpful, and I remember she would start off saying "Jeremiah used to do that" or "Jen, I know how you feel". It was her statements that made me feel like I was not alone. She understood. After she was aware of some of Elijah's ongoing behavioral challenges, she started reaching out more. She would share how she handled similar incidents involving her son. Since Elijah and Jeremiah are about 4 years apart, I felt like she had so much insight. Often, she would tell me about her meetings at the school to set up Jeremiah's accommodations and when a teacher was not abiding by his IEP. At times, these conversations were accompanied by tears, but she was always encouraged that things were going to work out.

Though different from my nursing school community, this felt similar. Someone who shared similar life circumstances as me and being transparent about the challenges we are facing together was refreshing. This community that was developing kept me from isolating myself. I allowed the enemy to whisper thoughts of doubt making me feel like I did something to cause his behavioral problems. This was a community of a different kind, but nevertheless a community evolving before me. It was one that I did not know that I needed, but it was on time.

In 2017, Red and her family relocated out of state. The current school system had not served her son well and she learned that other states had more resources to support Jeremiah such as speech therapist, diagnosticians, and case managers through the school district, which proved to be vital in the success of a child with a disability. Because of our friendship, it allowed us to create a community through the diagnosis that our sons share. This connection was the reason she was the first person I called when I realized Elijah was going through puberty and had all the evidence to prove it. I was mortified. I explained to her how I learned Elijah had pubic hair, she said, "Jen, I was the same way when Jeremiah was going through puberty". The community that we developed has been impactful. The thing that has been the most confirming in this community is that what God allows you to go through is not for you to overcome and keep to yourself. It serves as a gift of hope and strength of what God has brought you through to those that are going through a similar circumstance. If Red had not shared her experiences and struggles, I may have kept what I was going through with Elijah to myself. Had she not been transparent with me, I would not have felt open enough to discuss my feelings and the barriers we were facing. Community was everything and I know Jeremiah's diagnosis was not just for Red, but it was for me and my family as well. Red and I know the impact this diagnosis has on a first-time mom, just as we were when our sons were diagnosed. I do not think this was a coincidence. I think that our God is so loving and perfect, that He knew what she was going to need in the midst of her son's diagnosis, and she would have a community just for her. To prove this point, our mutual friend's firstborn has been diagnosed with Autism. God has allowed the three of us to do life together as friends. He is also making us victorious as we build our community of moms of children diagnosed with Autism. Knowing how much support our friend needs, we enveloped her into our community. We are developing a stronger bond as we lean on, pray, support, and encourage one another.

In 2014, life seemed to be passing me by as I went through the mundane routine that was never ending. Work, daycare pick up, dinner, bath time, play, then bedtime. This was my routine every single day. I did not make much time for my own quiet time, but I continued to go to church, but I was lonely. Marvin was supportive, and hard-working but quiet. Elijah was fun, energetic, happy, but exhausting. I needed my own people. I had friends; however, they were in different seasons of life, so I felt isolated because it felt as if no one would understand what I was going through. Marvin and I would have the occasional date night, but generally, things were the same during the week and church on the weekends.

I started to notice that Marvin began being gone more often when he was in town. It felt like he was gone at least three nights out of the week, doing something related to church. I appreciated that he was spending his time doing the work God had called him to, but it left me alone, which I started to resent him for and honestly was jealous, but I was not sure why. I had my own relationship with the Lord, but Marvin had every other week prison ministry on Fridays, was a CASA volunteer, and co-led a men's life group on Monday evenings. His time away allowed me to spend a lot of time with Elijah; however, I did not have anything that was something just for me, besides my job. It got to be where Marvin was not only going with these men for the scheduled things, but they were going to New Orleans to see the Saints play and going to LSU football games. There were times when I was angry with him because he had the audacity to have built a community to do life without me?!?! I am aware that is a completely selfish thought, and I should have been happy for him. This is how I felt but, this is also how I learned the enemy creeps in not only marriages, but relationships, through isolation. What I did not know until later, was that Marvin and the men in his life group had been praying for their wives to find life groups of their own. I did not realize how badly I needed a community, but I did know that I was becoming more isolated and craving adult interaction.

In 2015, we welcomed our daughter, Corynn, to our family. She was a tiny, precious girlish resemblance of Elijah, except with a lot less hair. She was a sweet baby, but she was much different than Elijah. Elijah was a quiet baby who rarely cried. Corynn on the other hand cried about everything. She did not like riding in the car. She did not like baths. She cried if you left her in the car seat for too long once we made it to our destination. Corynn did not like noises that interrupted the quietness that she enjoyed so she would cry. What Corynn did like was her mom and dad. When she was not crying, she would give the sweetest smiles that I interpreted as the joy that God was allowing me to have through her despite the feelings of darkness that I had been battling.

Before Corynn was born, the isolation that I was experiencing earlier in 2014, did not get any better, in fact, it got a lot worse. During my pregnancy with Corynn, I was diagnosed with hyperemesis gravidarum. What is that? It's when the morning sickness and vomiting persist throughout the entire pregnancy. This results in weight loss, dehydration, and multiple hospitalizations for IV fluids. Though I was not officially diagnosed while I was pregnant with Elijah, the symptoms were the same. It was worse this time because I knew what it was, and my OB/GYN took measures for this pregnancy to not be so debilitating. Despite having a subcutaneous Zofran pump for a few months and taking several medications, it did not stop me from having to be hospitalized during the pregnancy, put on bedrest for 2 months during the pregnancy, and ultimately removed from work six weeks before Corynn's delivery. It was during this time that the weight of the isolation became unbearable and tremendously heavy. I feel like I rarely saw Marvin and Elijah even though we were in the same apartment. The loneliness that was already there was compounded by the illness and the side effects from the medicines. The medications made me sleepy and most of the time it still did not stop me from vomiting. I was so disconnected from my family and felt like I could not be around Elijah because as an energetic 2-year-old, he did not understand that any movement caused me to become ill.

There was a time during the pregnancy that the isolation turned into a darkness that did not allow me to see my way out. It was a deep hole, where no light existed. This hole that I was in also came with very clear thoughts of taking my own life when I was alone, which was most of the time, especially when I was on bedrest. I felt like everywhere I looked, there was no light to be seen. This was scary because I felt like I could not control these thoughts. What I began to understand later as a believer in Christ was that "we must take captive every thought to make it obedient to Christ" as Paul tells us in 2 Corinthians 10:5. At that time, I was not equipped for this battle in my mind. I remember the phone call that I made to my mom that night. I realized for her to hear the thoughts that I spoke aloud had to be scary. I was driving around the city that rainy night, my eyes were filled with tears, and she was the only person that I felt I could tell. I know that conversation was scary for her because I could hear the tone change in her voice from mom to prayer warrior. She asked me a series of questions probing to see if I had a plan. Her compassion and love that night became the community that I needed at that moment and saved my life. She would not allow me to hang up until I made it upstairs, in my apartment, and safe. I am certain that she later made a phone call to Marvin to make him aware because I feel like he started to check on me more often. What my mom was for me that night is why *true* community is so important. It could be the difference between life and death.

A few weeks before Corynn was born, the thoughts subsided only for a short time. In the weeks leading to her birth I had somewhat of a euphoric feeling. There was going to be a new life and Corynn's birth meant that I could get back to some type of normalcy. However, because she was so different from Elijah, I quickly became sleep deprived as many moms of newborns are. The days seemed long with a now three-year-old and a newborn. Initially, I was just feeling exhausted and felt like a zombie, but those feelings of exhaustion slowly started turning into thoughts of darkness again. I had the life that others prayed for, and I had an overwhelming guilt for these thoughts because I felt like something was wrong with me. I would pray and the thoughts would go away for a little while, but it grew so much that I had to finally share with Marvin that I did not feel comfortable being alone. He did his best to support me through this time; however, I think he still did not understand the gravity of what I was struggling with. The sadness that lingered after I had Corynn was something that I needed to talk to someone about because the enemy was having a field day with me until I learned what it meant to take every thought captive. Since I was still in a place of isolation, this continued to be my struggle.

While I was on maternity leave, I had some quiet time while Corynn slept. When I wasn't doing laundry, nursing, or taking a nap, I began reading my bible. Specifically, when I started having these reoccurring thoughts, I would read God's word. It was then that I would see glimpses of His love for me. I realized in this season that I also had to focus my thoughts on Him. The more I focused on Him, I gained clarity and a stillness in my mind that I never recalled experiencing before. I started to think about things that were true, honest, pure, loving, and of a good report as Philippians 4:8 says. He always sent me what I needed when I needed it, as I started to slip back into feelings of isolation. In those instances, I would get an unexpected knock at my door. From my personal trainer to former nursing classmates, to a few of my friends, including Red. They showed up just when I needed them most. They were what my heart was desiring. I needed community. The Lord impressed on their heart to come and sit with me, which allowed me to refocus and to think on *these* things as Paul said. My community continued to change and grow, and during this season, it came through my answered prayers that showed up in the form of random visits from people who God sent to me. After their visits I felt so much better about the thoughts and the weight of the depression lifted the more I spoke. By the time each person would leave, I felt strong. The Lord provided me with the glimpse of hope and light that I needed to change my perspective. This was baffling to me how impactful having conversations and being around people was for not only my mood, but also my spirit.

Corynn and Elijah were getting older, and Marvin started traveling more with work, which allowed me to learn to manage my time better. After all, trying to balance a one- and four-year-old with a full-time job proved to be a challenge. I had friends that became my community to help with the kids when Marvin was out of town, and I had to work late. After all, we did not have any family that was nearby. They were truly a blessing, but I still had that gnawing feeling that something was missing. We had been at our church for a few years, and I had not connected with anyone yet. As someone who felt like I had the friends that I wanted, I did not feel the need to make new friends; however, I was not totally closed off to welcoming new people into my life. In this season, I prayed for something different. My prayer for God to lead me to like-minded people who understood me and loved me despite my flaws. I believe it was through my quiet time with God and the prayers of Marvin's life group that led me to my first life group. The invitation came from Danielle, the wife of one of the men in Marvin's life group. I did not know her well, but she was nice enough to extend an invitation to me, so I went. In this group were several women of different walks of life. Most had older kids, but a few were middle-aged with adult children. I learned a lot biblically in the short time in this group; however, the leader of the life group had to dissolve the group, so I was left without the community I prayed for. Though I would occasionally see the familiar faces of that life group when I attended church, I still knew I had to find a community that was for me. It was not long before the next life group came along because of the invitation from Danielle, yet again. It's amazing to me that until this time in my life, I never considered Genesis 2:18 to be outside the context of marriage; however, I know exactly what this meant. "It is not good for man to be alone. I will make a helper that is right for him" was why I was experiencing depression because I had isolated myself many times in my life for various reasons. Nevertheless, I was alone. I also remember how the enemy had tormented my thoughts because I positioned myself by myself.

I pulled up to Tiffany's house with the delicately landscaped front yard. It was welcoming, and I felt at ease waiting for the door to open. She opened the door with a bright smile. It was a much smaller group of ladies than the previous group, which I was okay with. I don't remember much about the lesson, but I just recall noticing how much I felt at home being here. Once it was over, I left and knew I would be back. I continued attending and had to start bringing Elijah and Corynn from time to time when Marvin was out of town. Those nights, I would come in feeling overwhelmed, and frustrated until I got inside. There was always so much peace in Tiffany's home. What I enjoyed most about this group was that they would meet up for coffee or beignet's randomly. These impromptu meetings allowed me to get to know some of the ladies better. One evening after life group, Tiffany invited me to join her and Danielle on their 6 am walks through their neighborhood. This was after the 2016 flood in Baton Rouge that left many homes in ruin. The paths on the sidewalks on every street were obstructed with all the debris from those reconstructing their homes. On these walks, I learned more about Tiffany and Danielle. I recall it was on these walks that I learned about the book club and was invited to attend the one that Danielle was hosting, which was *Made to Crave* by Lysa Terkeurst. Because I received the invite late, I did not have time to read the book. Honestly, I probably only read about half of most of the book club books because for me, it was all about being a part of a community.

I found myself thriving not only in my relationship with God, but in my marriage, and in my career since joining this life group that we later adopted the name B-Sisters. Through this group of ladies, I found friends that I knew I needed but had no clue to what they would bring to the life of me and my family. We did a lot of things that I did not realize I enjoyed. We did outreaches together. We supported a friend of Danielle that stepped out on faith and opened a storefront bakery together. We celebrated birthdays. We would randomly meet up for coffee after work. Some weekends we would spend time at the local farmer's market. I found myself laughing more and truly having joy. Our bond grew to the point that life group would last longer than just the allotted hour and a half. I would stay behind catching up with the ladies on my week and hearing about the things that were happening in their lives. This was what I enjoyed. I no longer felt the weight of loneliness, but the joy of community and friendship.

I had a little over a year of community with my B-sisters before me and my family left Baton Rouge and moved to Dallas, Texas in 2018. The thought of the isolation of being in a new place where I did not have an established community was not something I was looking forward to. I knew what I needed to thrive in my new city, it was community. Our goal was to first find a church home and then join a small group. I expected this to happen immediately, but to my surprise, there were way more churches that we visited than I could have imagined in the DFW metroplex. In fact, this did not happen for a while, but I was hopeful because I knew God was going to do exactly what He did for me in Baton Rouge, only better.

After being in Dallas for almost a year, the feelings of solitude were back. Despite my efforts to join a small group at the church where we were long-term visitors, I felt the sand slowly tipping the scale towards isolation. As my relationship with God was stronger now, I knew how to reach out to my established community and my B-sisters stayed in contact with me. During the first several months in Dallas, this community was important because I did not have local connections. My thoughts would sometimes waver, then through prayer, I would take those thoughts captive, wait and watch for glimpses of God's goodness. With things busier at work and at home, I leaned on these connections that I maintained with not only my B-sisters, but the book club as well.

I was asked to host our March 2019 book meeting, by Monica, the visionary for the book club. I chose *Becoming* by Michelle Obama as my book, so the only thing left was to secure a place since we lived in an apartment at the time. Little did I know that we would be relocating to Texas, so I thought I was off the hook for hosting. Once I moved, I would receive much needed calls from Monica while on my commute to work. These calls became more frequent and when it wasn't a call, it was a text that would necessitate a phone call later. From marital advice, to parenting advice, to business advice, it seemed like every situation that I was going through, Monica had been there and had the encouragement that I needed. Whatever it was that I needed at that time, God provided through Monica. She recognized that I had not found my community yet, but through her calls and the bond that developed between us, Monica became my community.

Of course, in typical Monica fashion, one of our conversations in January 2019 was her checking in to make sure I was still planning on hosting a book club in Dallas in the coming months. This call provided me with the opportunity to share with her that we had just purchased our first home and would have more than enough room to accommodate those that decided to take our book club on the road. However, this also meant that I was not off the hook, but I looked forward to connecting with the ladies again.

By the time March came around, I was in desperate need for the community that I had with the ladies. A few weeks prior to their arrival, I had felt overwhelmed and started to experience that heaviness that I couldn't control. It was that feeling of loneliness that continued to creep in; however, this time, I knew what this was. I was not alone. I had a community. I had a God who loves me. I was blessed with a loving, healthy family. I was victorious. I was victorious not only because I knew how to take these dark and negative thoughts captive, but victorious because I had people that God had place in my life that loved me despite my imperfections. This was my community. By the time book club came around, I was looking forward to the lady's arrival with so much anticipation. I treasured the weekend they spent at my home as it brought joy. This Dallas book club was the start of taking our book club on the road. After Dallas, we hosted our next book club at the beach in Alabama and then went international and did our book club on a cruise to Mexico.

Though no longer my life group or in the same state, these ladies were and still are my community. It is because of them that I had the courage to step out on faith to create a community for people around me. As much as I know I needed community, I realized it was time for me to be the community for others.

Because it is not God's intention for us to live life on our own. Isolation can and is dangerous. Isolation is darkness. Light cannot coexist with darkness. For some, I realize being around too many people can be overwhelming; however, seeking out relationships with people has been paramount to my success in navigating this life. Jesus did not live life alone, nor should we. Initially, time alone can be comfortable, but it can start to get uncomfortable and opens the door to the enemy to wreak havoc on your mind. This is why community is so important. The enemy will have you to believe things that are not true when you are in isolation. I learned that unity and connection with people through our shared experiences and circumstances whether it be a diagnosis or season of life is what debunks the lies the enemy will have us to believe. It is through our victory in Christ and within a community that we can live our best life. Through prayer, reading God's word, and stepping out on faith, I have victory through community.

"The hole in my heart is still there with no way to fill it, yet I had to find a way to turn that sadness into joy."

Victory Over Abuse and Grief

TAWANDA WEATHERSPOON

Growing up in an abusive household can have a seriously long-term effect on a child. Well, that is how I grew up! Witnessing abuse in so many aspects. Not just physical but mental, sexual, emotional, and verbal. I did not realize that the older I got, the more normal abuse became to me because of what I witnessed constantly for years.

1985, a senior in high school, playing on the girls' basketball team, I found myself pregnant just one month after turning 17. It was for my high school sweetheart. We were in love, or so I thought. I was left alone to deal with this. I was so scared to tell my mom. Even though she had divorced our family abuser by this time, the anger was still there, and I did not want her to take it out on me. One day, I was waiting for the doctor to call. When the phone rung, my mom and I both answered at the same time. It was my doctor calling to confirm that I was pregnant. When he said it, I screamed at the phone, and my mom screamed my name. She looked at me, and all she could do was cry. See, I was the baby of seven children. I remember praying, asking God to take this away. I did not want it. I was too young, I had my whole life ahead of me, and I was still in high school. I pleaded with God. I started going to church, having people pray for me, hoping by some chance God would hear them since He was not listening to me. I grew more and more angry with God. Why wasn't He listening to me! I saw people do far worse things than I did and they still received their blessing. Why can't you do this for me? I began seeing God as a punisher. Not loving towards me, but angry, upset, and disappointed in me. How do you recover from that? I felt as though I had fallen into the hands of an angry God, and He was going to dish out His punishment, and all I could do was deal with it. "Fine, I'll handle this myself"; that was the last thing I said to God. I did not talk to God for a long time. I went on to graduate high school. On May 25, 1986, I wobbled across the stage to receive my diploma. A few months later, on July 21, 1986, after 28 hours of hard labor, I gave birth to my beautiful baby boy. I named him Travis Anthony Weatherspoon. I was instantly in love with him. I had enough sense to ask God to forgive me for asking Him to take this baby away. Selfish request, I know!

About a year after I had my son, I met a man who was a sound and lighting technician for a local band in town. I would often go to hear this band play, and somehow, we started talking. We would talk for hours. We started hanging out more and talking on the phone more. After about three or four months, we started officially dating and quickly moved in together. Everything was going great. He worked at a local dry cleaners and I was working in fast food. I remember one day he came in from work angry. When I asked what was wrong, he yelled at me, and I yelled back. This is when the verbal abuse started. I did not even see it. It started small. An argument here and there. It quickly turned physical. I never even thought to talk to God. See, I was handling it myself. This is normal. This is what couples do, right! It only got worse. Some of the physical altercations I cannot remember. My family tried to help me, but I was so afraid I would not let them. Fear had gripped me, and I was paralyzed by it. I even convinced myself that they were trying to ruin my relationship. I just knew this was what love looked like. See, abuse was something I was familiar with and had unknowingly normalized. It was so dark in my life, and turning to the light never entered my mind. I never talked to God. I was afraid He was going to tell me to leave. I was still angry with Him because I had had a child and I couldn't go do what all my friends were doing. I could not go to college, parties, or travel like my friends were doing. I loved my son, but I wanted to have my cake and eat it too.

I faced the situation one day and asked the Lord to help me get out. I called a family friend in Atlanta, Ga, and asked him if I could move in with him until I got on my feet. I left my son with my mom, packed up my car on January 7,

1988, and moved to Atlanta, Georgia. **I Got Out**. Everything was going well for me. I would drive home every other weekend to see my son. Then I made the ultimate mistake! I let my abuser back into my life. I got an apartment, and he moved to Atlanta. I came back to Baton Rouge and got my son. We were going to be a family. I thought he had changed. We are in a new city, and this is a new opportunity for us to begin again. Being in a new city does not stop the violence. It just gives it a new home. Needless to say, the violence grew worse and worse. Now, I had no family to turn to. I was isolated, and he knew this. His abuse was always towards me, never my son.

I started talking to God, asking Him to help me again. Realizing how big of a mistake I made, I was scared. Sometimes, all I could say was, "Lord, help me." I did not wait to hear from God, I devised a plan. I did not tell anyone because I could not chance this man finding out. I would go to the bank this particular weekend and deposit the money my son and I would need to get away, and we would leave the next weekend while he was at work. When he went to work, I would call to make sure he was there, and then my son and I would jump in our car and head home to Baton Rouge to my mom's house. I knew he would be gone at least eight hours. *Time to activate the plan.* One Saturday morning, I went to the bank to make the deposit as planned. While at the bank, I started feeling anxious, scared, and uneasy. I thought it was my nerves. The bank teller looked at me and asked if I was okay. She said I did not look well. Aside from the effects of the abuse, the feelings I was having grew worse. I felt a sense of urgency to get home. I asked her if she could hurry because I need to go. When I arrived home and walked through the door, I heard my boyfriend screaming at the top of his lungs. I ran up the stairs. He was on the phone with 911 saying, "He fell! He fell!" My son was lying on my bed unresponsive. I PANICKED. He told me he fell and hit his head. I tried to give him CPR. In my haste, I picked him up and headed to the emergency room. The ambulance cut me off, stopping me, and immediately took my son. I followed behind them, not knowing what happened or what was going on with my child.

The trauma unit nurse at Grady Memorial Hospital whisked my baby away swiftly to examine him. They immediately put me in a room to wait. They would come and give me updates periodically. It was never good news, but I was hopeful. I prayed to God; I reasoned with God; I begged God; I even negotiated with God. The news about my son remained unfavorable. I grew more and more angry with God. I began quoting scripture of how Jesus raised the little girl from the dead (Matthew 9:24-25). I reminded Him of how He raised Lazarus from the dead (John 11:43). Why couldn't He heal my baby? What had he done to You? He was three years old. He deserves to live just like the woman from Shunem's son (2 Kings 4). She did not ask for her son either, but when her son died, You raised him from the dead. I thought You were no respecter of person. See, I knew scripture because I'm a preacher's child. I just did not walk in the way of the Lord and thought I could bend Him to my will. Foolish, I know. As I calmed down a bit from the adrenaline, I fell asleep. As I lay there, I had a dream that my son had come to me and told me, "Hey Mom, I'm going home." I jumped up and told him to give me a moment to gather my things. I heard him say, "No, Mom, I'm going home." I said, "Okay." When I went to grab him to hug him, my arms went through him like a ghost. I kept trying over and over again to hold on to him, but I couldn't. I was startled out of my sleep when I heard people running and yelling down the hall. I woke up thinking, "That's my son." I ran out of the room to see him, but they wouldn't let me in. They were trying to revive him for the fourth time. I waited in a small room right outside the children's ICU. About 30 minutes later, the nurse came out, and I knew. She looked at me, and I said, "It's okay." That is all I could say. She sadly said she was so sorry. See, he already told me he was going HOME.

My Precious Baby Boy Had Passed Away.
To be absent in the body is to be present with the Lord.

I looked up and asked God one more time, "Please raise my son from the dead." I tried to convince Him that I believed in miracles. See, though I am a preacher's kid, I did not have a relationship with God. I didn't know about reverence for God, serving God, having a relationship with Him, or loving Him for who He is and not for what He could provide. I did not desire a relationship with Him; I just wanted my son healed so I could go on with MY life. God has a way of bringing forth His will for us, and we must learn to trust in it. This may sound cruel, but if God had to bring one of us home, praise God, it was my son. See, I know he is in heaven with Jesus. Me? I would not have made it to Heaven, and I know that. I knew that in that moment. God and I have had this conversation. I wasn't living for Christ. I wasn't seeking Him or a relationship with Him. I was living for me. I was crying out to him but had no connection with Him.

After the nurse broke the news to me, they allowed me to go into the room and hold my son for a while. At that moment, the grieving began. I could feel anger rising in me, as I had to let my son go. My emotions ran wild. I screamed so loud, I scratched up my neck and arms. I had never felt pain like this, and I did not know what to do with it. I wanted to die right along with him. The devil tempted me with suicide so many times. I knew enough about God to know that that would separate me from Him and my son forever. I now had to contact my mom and my siblings and give them the most unbearable news ever. I had to tell them that what they feared for me, what they had hoped to prevent had happened. My son, her grandson, their nephew was dead, and I wasn't 100% sure of how it happened. I could only repeat his story. My father took care of all my son's funeral arrangements, including flying his body back to Baton Rouge, Louisiana. On March 10, 1990, my son passed away at Grady Memorial Hospital in Atlanta, Georgia. On March 17, 1990, we buried my three-year-old son at Winnfield Funeral Home in Baton Rouge, Louisiana, just four months short of his fourth birthday. That Monday, I returned to Atlanta to face my boyfriend.

The Truth Comes Out
Do not forget this piece of armor. It is important.

Three days after my son's funeral, that Tuesday, I received a phone call from the coroner's office asking me to come down to the hospital. When I arrived, they asked me to explain to them what happened to my son. I gave them the replay of the story based on what my boyfriend told me." So you weren't there when it happened?" the officer asked me. "No sir, I was at the bank. When I got home, I found my son lying across my bed unconscious!" "Can you prove your whereabouts?" the officer asked. "Yes, I still have my bank deposit slip." The officer looked at me and said, "Ma'am, I'm afraid your son didn't just fall and hit his head!" Okay, so what are you telling me?" He went on to tell me that my son was hit in the forehead. That the swelling of his brain was due to the injury sustained to his forehead. "He did, in fact, fall backward and hit a hard object, but the blow to the front of the head is what killed your son." The anger in me is rising as this conversation goes on. I am screaming to the top of my lungs. "He told me he fell; he told me he fell. Why would he do this to my son? He's innocent, he can't hurt you, and he's three years old." The whole time during this interview, they kept whispering to one another. I am in shock because this is not making sense to me. By the time I made it back to my apartment, with intentions of seeking revenge in some way, they had arrested my boyfriend and charged him with the murder of my son. I learned that they wanted me to come down to the hospital not only to answer questions and tell what they discovered but also to remove me from the home while commencing the arrest. They did not want him to do anything to me when they came to arrest him. I never went to court because I could not fathom the thought of someone doing this to a child, let alone *my* child, or to hear the details of what he did. He was notorious for abusing me, but not my son. I don't know how much time he received, but I know the judge convicted him of manslaughter.

Two months later, I decided to drive to South Carolina to go to the beach. While in the water, I began feeling sick. Something was not right, and I knew I needed to get to the doctor. What I feared the most came upon me. Yes, I was pregnant. I was carrying the baby of the man who murdered my son. Again, I prayed and asked God if he would fix this. How was I now going to tell my family this on top of everything else we were dealing with? I felt like I needed to check into a mental facility because I was breaking, falling rapidly, and I could not stop. I felt like God's anger was coming back up against me again. I told God, even Job caught a break, Jonah was spit out, Daniel was not eaten, and the three Hebrew boys didn't even have the smell of smoke in their clothes. Please help me, God. Little did I know He heard me. About two months after finding out, I was pregnant and sharing the news with my family, God spoke to me, *"It's not this child's fault!"* That is all he said. I simply looked up and said okay. About five months later, two of my sisters showed up in Atlanta, Ga with a U-Haul truck, and packed me up to bring me back to Baton Rouge, Louisiana. I did not hesitate; I simply trusted that this was the right thing to do. I called my job and told them I was leaving in two days to move back home. They transferred me to a position in Baton Rouge.

My Journey With God Begins
He is the way, the only way.

Coming back home to Baton Rouge was tough. I felt the anger, hatred, and bitterness towards me, the shame and embarrassment I brought into my family. Many days, I would put on a brave face around people. However, if they verbally attacked me, I fought back, and if they criticized me, I dug up their past and handed it right back to them. I lost so many friends over this. I was so exhausted from fighting. I felt like I had fought all my life. I drove to my grandmother's house in Clinton, Louisiana, to visit her and my aunt. When I saw them, I just collapsed in my grandmother's lap. She told me, "Baby, we all have a past, but I'm not going to beat you up. I'm sorry this happened to you, but I love you." My aunt just gave me the biggest hug and told me to get on in the house and go eat. Abuse will wear you down; see, many types of abuse visited my life: physical, verbal, sexual, mental, and emotional. Not all at the same time, but some would come together. Not to mention the battle I had with self-hatred, feelings of rejection, and feelings of abandonment. I had had enough. I aimed to win at all costs. I will not lose anymore. I prayed to God, "Lord, before I lose another child at the hands of man, please get me out of the situation." Before I go any further, let me say this: that was the dumbest prayer I could have ever prayed. However, I was tired, so I prayed what I thought was a good prayer. I started going to church, learning the word, and trying to build this relationship with God that I knew I needed and wanted. On December 5, 1990, Antoine Tre'vez Weatherspoon was born. I was in love all over again. I vowed this one would be different. I would protect him at all cost, I would raise him in the true word of God, and he would grow up knowing how much I loved him. He would never doubt my love, feel rejected, or alone. I read in the bible that God would rather you not vow than to vow and not keep it. (Ecclesiastes 5:5 - It is better to say nothing than to make a promise and not keep it.) Mentally, I knew what I said, and I was not going back on it for no one. "A wound can't heal with a band aid on it." Even though I have my son Antoine, there were moments I would be driving by myself, and I would hear Travis in the back seat of my car talking to me like he used to do. He would come to me in my dreams and tell me he is okay and that he would see me again. That statement really put me on the path of seeking Jesus. I went to the altar one morning at church and simply said, "LORD, I FORGIVE HIM." Constantly repeating, "I forgive him." That was the easy part. Now, to walk out that forgiveness. I made my second vow to God. I will not look at Antoine as a replacement for Travis, I will not cause Antoine to pay for the wrongs of his father, I will not criticize his father in front of him, I will raise him as Antoine not Travis, and when the time come, I will tell him the truth.

A year after having my second son, I met someone. We started out just talking and occasionally going out. About two months later, we started dating. I met his family, and he met mine. I knew after a year that this was not going to work, but I stayed anyway. I even moved in with him. Classic Tawanda. Remember that prayer I prayed, "Get me out"? February 1993, we got engaged. I went to my mom's house to show her and my sister the ring. I mustered up as much excitement as I could, but my sister saw right through it. It was going to be a quick engagement. The wedding date is set for June 12 1993. Every day, I wrestled with marrying this man. See, I was back in a similar situation like Atlanta. All the signs were there. It started out verbal like before. This time, I was guarded. I alerted two of my sisters about the things that were going on. Nevertheless, I still stayed. In April 1993, I went to the altar and gave my life to the Lord. At that moment, he changed drastically and started using the bible against me. Prior to me going to the altar in April, I became sick. I looked up to the Lord and simply said, "Not again!" I realized that I had created a pattern in my life, and it was not the one God had for me. I was so busy being angry; I did not see how the enemy was using that to his benefit. BUT GOD! May 12, 1993, I called off the engagement. Exactly one month before the wedding. I moved my son and me out of that apartment and back to my mom's house. Not knowing I was pregnant at the time. I was thanking God for honoring my prayer, but I was still trying to work things out with him. I was trying to change him myself. One day in August 1993, we had a physical fight in the parking lot of one of our friends' apartments. Yes, while I was pregnant with his child. The difference this time around, he was arrested and charged with the death of a fetus, and I was in the emergency room at the local hospital. The hospital was monitoring me to see if my baby was okay. I remember lying in that hospital bed praying and asking God to fix this. He heard me! He heard my cry for my baby. To God be all the glory, she survived, and five months later, on January 6, 1994, I gave birth to the most beautiful little girl, Taylor Ann Weatherspoon. She was born healthy and strong. It was at this moment I came to realize how dumb that prayer was that I prayed. What my prayer should have sounded like was, "Lord, please keep me from ever going into another situation like this ever again. Give me wisdom and discernment to see the enemy and to flee from him." However, God still delivered me and my children out of the enemy's trap. Hearing God's voice and obeying the leading of the Holy Spirit is so important to our daily lives. His leading and guiding me to walk away from that engagement was a lifesaver for me, my children, and for the guy as well.

God began dealing with me about my attitude, my behavior, and my character. He showed me how they mimicked generational curses that were over my family. He taught me about soul ties. When you are intimate with others, you can take on those spirits they possess. He began showing me how I was taking on some of those character traits of the men I had been involved with; things like constant anger, a lying spirit, and manipulation, just to name a few. I was so hurt when I realized what I did to myself and how that made God feel. I would do whatever it took to get me through or out of situations. I just did not care because I felt like no one cared about me. I often say, "God watches over fools and babies," and I was not a baby. I was praying one night and said to the Lord, "I break those curses from over me and my children and my children's children to the fourth and fifth generations." I taught my children to pray that same prayer as well until Jesus returns. God had me calling out, binding up, and casting down spirits like divorce, lying, cheating, murder, anger, pride, incest, adultery, lust, bitterness, hatred, etc. Then he had me loose agape love, husband of one wife over my son, wife of one husband over my daughter, a spirit of truth, a spirit of humility, obedience to the word of God, godly friends for my children, that they would cultivate a covenant relationship with Jesus/Holy Spirit, forgiveness, and so much more. This journey continues to this day. I'm learning to always look to God first, listen for His voice, and do what he says do. It all works for my good, after all. I have stumbled quite a few times on this journey, but He's always there to pick me up and get me back on the right path (Psalm 23:4, your rod and staff).

Walking in Forgiveness
Forgive, but never forget. It is your testimony to help someone else.

Forgiveness can be one of the most difficult things to do. I know it has been for me. The most important person I had to forgive was me. Michael Jackson said it best, "Starting with the man in the mirror." As I walked down my own path of forgiveness, I was able to begin forgiving others and allow my healing to begin. With the many situations I have been in in my life, I had to forgive myself for being rebellious, prideful, ignorant, stubborn, ungrateful, careless, willing, and hardheaded. In my heart, I knew these situations were wrong. The problem was that I did not know how to get out. I had never seen anyone truly get out. I saw them change partners, but never truly free. So I thought, well, this must be the way you adult in life. To forgive others is for your sake, not theirs. Release them so God can begin to work on your healing. This is what I had to do. I had to let go and let God take the wheel. God has shown me that through all the trials and tribulations I have been through, He was right there with me all the time. Yes, I lost my son, but he is in heaven. Now, because I live for Christ, I will get to see him again. That does not close up the hole in my heart, but it sure keeps the joy of the Lord bubbling up in my spirit. I still get up sometimes and say, "Lord, I forgive me, and I thank you for forgiving me as well." The enemy always tries to attack my mind, but I have the word of God to shut him up, to encourage myself, and confess God's love for me. I have learned and am continuously learning to pray for those who hurt me, no matter how great or small the offense may be. Prayer is my weapon over warfare, but it sometimes is my struggle. I have to remind myself and declare over myself, "Lord, I trust You, and I do not have anything to put my trust in but You. I do not have anyone else I can do this with, but You. No one else can lead, guide, guard, create, develop, protect, and orchestrate my life. All I have and want is You." I thank the Lord for His patience with me because my salvation walk has tested the best of Him. His love is so overwhelming. Sometimes I sit and cry when I think about how much He cares for me, and then I read it in His word how great, how wide and how deep His love is for me. He cares for me even when I don't care for myself. Now that is real love!

Walking in Victory
To walk in victory, there has to be a battle.

Three years after my son's death, I decided that I would not work on his birthday, that I would spend it remembering him and all the things we used to do together. Therefore, on July 21 of every year, I would go and do the things we once liked to do together. Things like, go watching airplanes land and take off at the airport, go ride bikes, or just go for a walk. In the beginning, I would cry a lot while doing these things, asking God why, wishing I could hold him again, give him a hug or just hear him say, "Hey, Mommy," one more time. It has now been 30 years since I started honoring him in this way. I remember praying one day before I started walking, and I just so happen to look down at my son's picture. I went and got a pencil and wrote his name down, Travis Anthony Weatherspoon, T. A. W. He and I have the exact same initials. Then it hit me like a ton of bricks (soft bricks, of course). Take A Walk. This is what I have been doing. I have been taking a walk in his honor. Therefore, I started calling it "National T. A. W Day." I was so excited that God gave me this. I felt like He saw Me that day and He loved Me so much that He gave this to Me. I was filled with so much joy that all I could do was cry happy tears at that moment. I looked up to heaven and thanked God. My walk that day was so amazing. I walked the Mississippi River levee for miles. I did not cry while I walked, I smiled a lot, I talked to people, and I even shared why I was walking with a woman who had no clue who I was, but she listened and said, "God bless you." I typically walk about 3 miles. Over the years, National T. A. W. Day has grown. My family is a huge supporter. Depending on where everyone is on that day, at some point they will Take A Walk. My children, my siblings and their families, my cousins, and all of my friends around the world now participate in National T. A. W. Day. Sometimes they come and walk with me. It really depends on what day of the week it falls on. Some will walk on their lunch break, after work, before work, while on vacation, etc. My brother had a friend who wanted to join in on the walk one year, but he had to work all day. Therefore, he decided to walk from his house to his car and from his car into his office for work. I thought that was so sweet, but funny too. I have friends and friends of friends, co-workers, family members and friends of family members who are literally around the world that take time out of their day to join me and walk on July 21. It is such a blessing. I always ask that while they are walking to take a moment to pray, have a moment of gratitude, to be thankful, to laugh, and to give God glory for all He has done for them. As I said, this walk happens all around the world. I have walked in New York, Chicago, Hawaii, New Zealand, Texas, Maine, Australia, or wherever I am on July 21. I think I have walked in 32 of the 50 states. I have even walked in Atlanta, Georgia, where this tragedy took place. My friends and family have walked in London, Switzerland, Japan, Germany, Scotland, the Netherlands, and Canada, to name a few. Because I was a former athlete, running and walking have always been a joy for me. I truly feel like I think clearer, my lungs are definitely getting stronger, and I am more relaxed afterwards. This walk is a double blessing. I run and walk to exercise as well.

The hole in my heart is still there with no way to fill it, yet I had to find a way to turn that sadness into joy. God gave me National T. A. W. Day. I now claim victory over grief. I don't spend my time anymore trying to understand the "why" behind how my life has been. I am learning to trust in God's perfect plan for my life, to listen to His voice, and take captive the crazy thoughts the enemy tries to throw at me or attack me with! There are still areas in my life where I need to allow God to come in and bring complete healing, and to help me fully trust Him no matter what. I used to think that God was an "I'm going to get you" God, that He is just going to abuse me or let me down as others have in the past. I know in my heart that that is not who He is, and He would never do that to me/us. He is a good, good father. Unfortunately, we live in a sin-cursed world. One day, God will make all this right again. Until then, we need to focus on the fact that we have a God who can turn horrible situations into beautiful redemptive moments that glorify His name. He brings beauty out of ashes. As we learn to surrender our hurts and desires to Him, we will stand in awe as we experience the freedom, peace, and victory He has been offering us all along. Remember, "A woman who kneels before God, can stand before anything."

July 21, 2026, will mark the day my son would have turned 40 years of age. My hope is to have 40,000 people around the world join me on National T. A. W. Day, not just to honor my son but also to rejoice about the things God has done in their own lives. I want everyone to celebrate how they have victory. (Anyone interested in capturing their special moments that day and sharing their photos on social media should use #NationalTAWDay2026.)

Epilogue

As we reach the conclusion of our shared journey through these pages, it is evident that each story, unique in its victory and triumph, weaves together two profound threads: At the heart of every victory lies the unwavering hope found in faith, and the journey to get there is strengthened by the presence of a compassionate and supportive community.

It is our heartfelt prayer that within these stories, you've found echoes of hope that resonate deeply within your heart and soul. In moments of solitude, though you may feel isolated, remember that you are always in the comforting embrace of something greater than you. The presence of the Almighty, a constant anchor and gentle guide, is never far away, offering relief and understanding in your times of need. This enduring truth is captured in the scripture, 'But thanks be to God! He gives us the victory through our Lord' (1 Corinthians 15:57).

Beyond the embrace of faith in Jesus Christ, the power of community stands as a testament to our shared experiences. In each other, we find a mirror of our struggles and a celebration of our triumphs. As it is wisely said, 'Two people are better off than one, for they can help each other succeed' (Ecclesiastes 4:9).

Our closing prayer for you is one of peace and enduring hope, found in both your spiritual journey and the embrace of a comm**UNITY** that uplifts and supports you through all seasons of life. Together, in faith and fellowship, we discover the keys to a life lived victoriously. We celebrate our victories and look forward with joy to the triumphs that await you.

Meet the Authors

MONICA GOREE

Monica is a native of St. Louis, Missouri and has lived in Baton Rouge, Louisiana since 1997. She is married to Donald Goree and they have two children; one son Brennan Goree, one daughter Brandi Goree, daughter-law Kylea Goree two precious grandchildren Brycen & Kamryn Goree. She is an alumna of Southeast Missouri State University, where she obtained her bachelor's degree in business marketing. In addition, she is a certified Mental Health Coach who enjoys mentoring young married couples and families. She has served on various boards throughout her community. Her core values include loving God, serving others, and leading by example. She is committed to being a lifetime learner and uses every opportunity to encourage and build people. When she is not working, she enjoys traveling, game nights with family & friends and reading a good book.

DANIELLE MACK

Danielle Mack is a dynamic professional known for her unwavering commitment to excellence and her vibrant personality. She is an accomplished leader in philanthropy and a passionate advocate for health equity and access and making a difference in the fight against cancer.

Danielle serves on various community organization and national boards, sharing her expertise and insights. Her outstanding contributions have earned her national and local recognition, including being named a member of the Forty Under 40 class by the Greater Baton Rouge Business Report and receiving honors from the Association of Healthcare Philanthropy and the Greater Baton Rouge Chapter of the Association of Fundraising Professionals.

Passionate about empowering women in philanthropy, Danielle plays a pivotal role as a mentor for the Women's Impact Initiative cohort, shaping and guiding the next generation of female leaders in the fundraising profession.

Outside of her professional endeavors, Danielle finds joy in exploring new cuisine and traveling with her husband, James. Together, they support their talented daughter, Autumn, a dedicated competitive gymnast.

JOYCE WEATHERSPOON-TALBERT

Joyce Weatherspoon-Talbert is a prolific writer, lauded director, and compassionate healthcare professional. Residing in Baker, Louisiana with her husband, she is actively involved in her church and ministers at the local Battered Women's Shelter, spreading the Gospel of Jesus Christ. She is the proud mother of one amazing daughter and enjoys spreading the love and passion of Christ to others.

TIFFANY COLEMAN

Servant Leader, Wife, and Mother, Tiffany Coleman, earned her Bachelor's in Business Management, a Master's in Nonprofit Administration, and paralegal certification. In addition to serving two decades in the legal and medical industries, she currently advocates for the needs of the community as a Grants Development Specialist in the nonprofit sector. Tiffany is passionate about her work and the blended family she has created with her husband, Lorenzo Coleman Sr. Mrs. Coleman loves spending time with her husband, family, and friends; but most of all, she loves serving God. Tiffany views the trials of her life as pruning and cultivation for her purpose. She strives to be a Proverbs 31 wife and mother, while answering the call to servant leadership.

LISA COLLINS

Lisa Collins, a St. Louis, MO native, has been residing in New Orleans since 2003. The proud mother of one incredible daughter, graduated college in 2022 and is now living her best life! The fearless storyteller has worked in various management positions in Corporate America for over 30 years. In 2016, Lisa became the Founder and CEO of Collins Accounting Services Group, LLC, a New Orleans-based company, with both national and international clients. When she is not crunching numbers for her clients, she enjoys reading, traveling, and taking advantage of the various food and music festivals throughout New Orleans.

DANIELLE ANDERSON

Born in Baton Rouge, LA, Danielle Anderson has been the proud wife of Marcus Anderson since 2006 and the mother of three incredible children, Diamond, Jalyn and Marcus Jr. She is the business owner of Pretty Girls & Co. and serves as a Middle School Teacher in Baker, La. Danielle's passion is serving those who are overlooked by demonstrating the love of Christ to all she encounters.

TIFFANY TEMPLE

Tiffany Temple lives in Baton Rouge, LA, loves Jesus and is a mother of one wonderful son, Triston Lee Brown. She enjoys all things family, crafty and pampering. Everything she has committed herself to, personally and professionally, has been driven by her desire to make a difference in the lives of women and children. When she's not spending time with her family and friends, you'll find her treasure hunting in locally owned stores or adventure-seeking off the beaten path.

BETTY LODGE

As the 9th child of 12 children reared in the small town of Jonesville, LA; Betty Lodge is a dynamic servant leader, mentor to women, and women's bible study enthusiast. She has been the proud wife of Freddie Lodge, Jr. for forty years and together they have two children, Angelica and Aaron. Mrs. Lodge is also the bonus mom to Marvin and Rochelle, a grandmother to six and great-grandmother of one. She is also excited about her new grandson who will arrive in February, 2024. The powerful speaker earned her Bachelor's degree in Secondary Education with an emphasis in Business Administration from Southern University of Baton Rouge in 1979. While balancing her family and ministry to women, Mrs. Lodge is the Director of Finance Operations in the healthcare industry in Baton Rouge. Because of her passion for women, children, single mothers, and the homeless, she served on a homeless shelter board in her community. Seeing women and children have a relationship with the Lord, and living a successful and fulfilling life with all opportunities available to them is her passion. As an author, Mrs. Lodge specializes in enriching, inspiring, and encouraging by providing hope and faith to all.

VALARIE DOWNING

For the past 25 years, Valarie Downing has been involved in women's ministry at various levels, using her passion for Christ to enhance the lives of women through the Word of God. She is a loving and devoted wife and mother of three adult children. She resides in Baton Rouge, Louisiana with her husband where she enjoys travel, reading, and family time.

JENNIFER TAYLOR

Jennifer Taylor is a Texas resident, but a South Louisiana girl at heart. She has been married to her college friend and sweetheart, Marvin, for 16 years. They share two sweet, inquisitive children, Elijah (11) and Corynn (8). Jennifer accepted the call to nursing and has dedicated the last 12 years to serving and caring for not only her patients but the teams that she leads as well. As a working mom, wife, and leader, Jennifer also serves as Elijah and Corynn's assistant, chef, housekeeper, and chauffeur. When there is spare time between practices, games, and music lessons, Jennifer enjoys spending time with her family and loves an opportunity for a self-care day at the spa. She started a dual graduate program in executive nurse leadership and business administration in the Fall of 2021. With this new endeavor, she strives to equip herself for whatever doors God chooses to open for her in the future. When there is a random quiet moment between semesters and her family is gone, she enjoys doodling scriptures in modern calligraphy. She hopes to continue experiencing life, and all that it brings with her family and friends, making deeper connections, and supporting one another through love, transparency, and community.

TAWANDA WEATHERSPOON

Mom of three, grandmother of two, entrepreneur, graduate of Baton Rouge Community College, and daughter of the King, Tawanda Weatherspoon, is a Regional Bond Supervisor with over two decades of experience in the Surety Bond Industry, serving several large construction contractors in the State of Louisiana. Tawanda is currently pursuing a new role of Surety Bond Manager across the footprint of the entire company.

In her spare time, Tawanda loves to crochet (T-Birds_Creations on Instagram) and travel to experience different cultures around the world. One way is through local coffee shops. Her motto is, "You can learn a lot in a coffee shop when chatting with the locals." She enjoys traveling so much she started her own travel agency, TAW Worldwide Travel, LLC, in honor of her late son. Having traveled around the world, she wants to assist others in experiencing that same joy and seeing the many wonders of this world.

Tawanda is a gifted encourager who is passionate about helping women see and know, "She is enough," because God says so.

"If sharing my truth will help someone, deliver someone, or encourage someone, then let the TRUTH be told."

THE SHADES OF VICTORY SISTERHOOD

(from left to right)
Danielle Anderson, Monica Goree, Jennifer Taylor, Betty Lodge, Danielle Mack, Joyce Weatherspoon-Talbert, Tawanda Weatherspoon, Lisa Collins, Tiffany Temple, Tiffany Coleman, Valarie Downing

Originating in October 2014, Shades of Victory Book Club emerged as a transformative sisterhood, providing a secure space for women to gather, exchange ideas, and embark on a journey of personal growth and empowerment. Our initial focus revolved around faith-based books, which played a pivotal role in our spiritual growth. However, our thirst for knowledge led us to explore diverse genres, allowing us to delve into leadership techniques, family dynamics, and social and emotional issues.

Through our shared passion for reading, we forged deep relationships that extended beyond the club's confines. Our bonds strengthened as we ventured beyond the pages, embarking on exciting adventures, from traveling and shopping to attending movies, and various activities that brought us joy. As a tightly-knit community of genuine friendship, we take pride in celebrating one another's victories and providing unwavering support during challenging times. It is our shared experiences and the commitment to navigating life together that has solidified the foundation of this sisterhood, holding us together for almost a decade.

As we approach our remarkable tenth anniversary, we sought to commemorate this milestone by sharing our personal life experiences and tales of triumph. Our heartfelt desire is that those who read our anthology will find solace, connection, and encouragement within our stories. We hope our narratives resonate deeply with readers, offering them a sense of inspiration along their journeys.

Made in the USA
Columbia, SC
09 February 2025

53510591R00078